Clive Norman

My Symbiont and Me

Limited Special Edition. No. 8 of 25 Paperbacks

Born in 1950, in the quaint village of Alfriston in East Sussex, England, United Kingdom, nestled between hills in the Cuckmere valley, the author had a magical childhood roaming the hills, meadows, river banks and wooded landscapes with his two brothers and friends.

He has always been very spiritual in nature and in 1972, due to circumstances beyond his control, he was left in both physical and mental pain, which was only to be aggravated and amplified later, following the breakup of his marriage in 1988. Since then, he has lived an extremely solitary life, and for 30 years has devoted himself to the pursuit and search for the truth of the one true reality and the peace within – ending his personal sufferances and beyond.

He has, for the last two years, been in retreat, in isolation, not leaving his home, where eleven months ago poetry started to stream from his mind, flowing like the beautiful clear waters of an underground mountain spring, bursting forth into the radiant light of the dawning sun.

A special dedication to Stuart and Mary Jenner

Clive Norman

My Symbiont and Me

Austin Macauley Publishers™
London • Cambridge • New York • Sharjah

A CIP catalogue record for this title is available from the British Library.

ISBN 9781528985024 (Paperback)
ISBN 9781528985031 (ePub e-book)

www.austinmacauley.com

First Published (2020)
Austin Macauley Publishers Ltd
25 Canada Square
Canary Wharf
London
E14 5LQ

I want to acknowledge the kind assistance of Lee Johnson, administrator of the “Free as a Bird Poetry” group on Facebook, and all my Facebook friends.

Table of Contents

"Social and Miscellaneous"

"Spiritual"

"Love and Romance"

Drifting Snow

I've missed you, my love
As the drifting snow
Right up high to the level
Of my beating heart
And perhaps my older smile.

As I count down the days
Of my dreams and imaginings
With foresightedness, forefront of my mind
And the fulfilment of our love
And many, many, shared embraces.

In a heavenly bliss, I've never felt
Or experienced before
Until our chance meeting
Beneath the starry skies
On a romantic moonlit evening.

When we strolled as one beneath the twinkling stars
Hand in hand as they winked at us, approvingly
In wave upon wave, riding upon the saddled moonbeams
Drifting, drifting down, down as white as snow
To the envy of young lovers everywhere.

How Mr Moon uses his experiences to guide
Our sincerest love that could ever be
With his beaming smiles and shiny rays

To watch consensually the joining embraces
Of two hearts, into an amazing, amazing togetherness.
Whilst he sings with a delightful harmony
In harmonious raptures and overtones
Rivalling any dawn chorus, sending love, through the air
In waves to the birds that doth sing
To the romanticised beat of love birds, holding hands.

Harmonious Love

Sit down beside me
Or upon my lap, my love
Rest your weary head
Down upon my shoulder.

Let me put my loving arms around you
To cuddle, to comfort you with extraordinary offerings
Your hand in mine, mine in yours
The wondrous feelings, sensual touches.

To touch, to share one's love enduring
Life forces exchanging, running through and through
Electrically charged auric particles flowing swiftly
Unexpectedly sharing an extra special, special kind of loving bonded gift.

You are my life, my one true love
Together we dance a very, very happy tune
Through cycles of life, a sweet embrace
Togetherness in harmony, becoming one.

Hearts Alive

Hearts alive, singing and dancing
Laughing and playing, rejoicing springtime
Fairies dancing amongst snowdrops
Frog jumping while crocuses uncoiling

Emerging, out, out, warming soils
Sunlight's gifted, unclouded skies.

Love permeating throughout airwaves
Infectious uninhibited, natural urges
Springing and prancing, dancing
Rapturous waves of irrefutable exuberances
Springs arrived, a cycling season
Evolutionary connotations ripen today.

Daffodils blooming, imitating sunshine
Warming hearts and souls alike
Alive, alive, a joy to be alive
Sap rising, while birds are singing
Up, up, up on high, birds' eyes
Viewing natures unfolding, beauty unbounded.

Feathers pruned, in placed perfections
Courtship dancing, awash, in harmonious
Ceremonial delights paraded
Flower buds breaking out
Reaching up, up into heavenly blue skies
Blooming, nurturing, embracing lovers sweetening
exploding hearts – everywhere!

My Clemantie

Mon chéri, my Clemantie
My dreams, my wishes
Are all of you, my treasured love
For I am yours, and you are mine
Forever and a day.

I am not a wealthy man
No materialistic wealth to speak of
Though my loving gift to you
Is so precious, so rare
Of spirituality, beyond compare.

With every touch, upon your cheeks, beautiful
Upon your lips and body too
In sweet embraces, of such loving warmth
Tenderness, enriching, heavenly blessed
A gifted rarity, you'll be smiling, smiling, forever, evermore.

The gift, of faithfulness, my adoring tenderest love
And enduring affectionate passions, too
All yours, to have, to hold, to cherish with every loving
embrace, to hug, to touch, to enrich
My gift to you, as our souls entwine, in heartfelt love
A radiance of spiritualities, flowing energies, spiritually
enhanced desires, especially for you – dearest Clemantie!

My Love for You

It was a magical moment when we first did meet
On a beautiful, sunny but late spring morning
The cherry blossoms blowing around and around
Like little butterfly confetti upon the wing.

It has been a year, a year, now my love
Since we first did meet while my thoughts have never waned
or wandered
From the special love I have for you
Always return to wondrous, beautiful thoughts of you.

If you give me your heart, so warm, so tender
My heart, my soul, my body will be forever yours
And the fears and anxieties you once did have
Will dissipate into mist, quickly fading upon the sweetest of
breezes.

It is your hand in marriage I ask of you, now, upon my
bended knees
For I will always love and be true to you until the heavens
fall soundly asleep

Leaving our arms wrapped around one another Entwined in loving embraces, forever and a day.

My Pulsating Heart

My pulsating heart racing, racing
Streaming hormones, around, and around in zestful enthusiasm

Chemical rampaging gusto es through, and through
Igniting passions and wondrous thoughts allowed.

Stimulated sensual desires, now running wild
Feelings of intimacy and uncontrollable urges
Arms wide open, waiting, waiting, your pacifying indulgences

Passionate urges, uncontrollable emergences, flowing swiftly, swiftly…

For you, my loving angel, my one, my only
Untainted, unwavering love's perfections
Forever yours, yours alone
You're my love, my heart's – sweetest desire.

The Swaying Wheat

I love to lie there smiling
Amongst the gently swaying, swaying wheat
Blowing casually around and around, in soothing flurries to the warming summer breeze
Whilst hidden, camouflaged, out of sight of prying eyes of intermittent passers-by.

What fun it is, making shapes of animals
From amongst the drifting fluffy passing clouds, floating slowly, slowly, by and by
So many, many unique, naturally occurring shapes

Invented, up there, there, in the heavenly, heavenly skies above.

Where lapwings hover, protecting young while singing a cheery song
Calling us, maybe, venting approvingly, from on high
Above the graceful eloquently swaying wheat, waving, waving, to the angels' fluttering hearts
In the fields to the lee side of the hill.

Many, many happy hours spent smiling, laughing all the while
Holding hands casually, not a hint, dream, or thought of more
Always treasuring, those guarded, secretive, extraordinary moments
Together, lying amongst the swaying, swaying, waving happy wheat, holding hands – with you!

Walk with Me

Come, take my hand
And walk with me
Leave your dithering heart
Behind; doubts you may have
But rest assured
I'll silence them, with loving tenderness.

The warming breeze
Gentile than I thought it'll be
Is very pleasant as we stroll along
Chatting, laughing, all the while
Like young lovers do
Everywhere.
May I embrace you now
With loving tender care
To hold you in my arms
Beneath this grandeur's old oak tree

To kiss you first, upon your blushing cheek
To whisper sweet nothings gently in your ears.

How my heartbeats, faster, faster like a drum
Now I've kissed you upon your rosy red cheeks
As my spirited expectations rise within
With gleefully hopeful anticipation, maybe
The stuff of dreams and imaginings
In the shelter of my warm, cosy bed.

“Prayer”

A Simple Prayer

My Lord and Master
Please hear this my prayer to you
Guide my footsteps carefully
As I journey life’s highways and byways
Through life’s torturous adventures.
As I walk my outward-bound journey
And the rocky road, I oft’ fear to tread
As my destined unknown passage, unfolds
Before me, into this chaotic world
Known only to me as the manifested plains.

Grant me; I beseech you
This one wish of mine
I need it, not for self-gratification
Or for self-righteousness
To serve my own egotistically delusional mind.
Please, please, grant me the abilities
To love as you do, with a much
Compassionate heart, always walk mindfully, as you do
Master
In the true spirit of loving-kindness
And the wisdom and worthiness of the ancients, of old.

Let me write as you dictate
The freely flowing words from out of my head
And out of the mouths of babes
To the paper, neither faltering or with hesitation
Whilst scribing God’s/Allah’s sacred words.

For just one solitary purpose
I beg you, beg you, to grant me, my prayer
To plant one, or a few, good seeds
In the minds of young children, now
To grow to fruition, to blossom and to serve thee well.

Devil Begone

Devil begone, begone
I have danced to your sombre listless tunes
For far, far, too long with your idiotic whimsicalities
It's my turn now, now, to walk the walk
Beat my drum, forcing the pace
Challenging you and your bittersweet
Twisted notions of heaven.

Begone, I say, begone
Dance to your own pitiful, nocuous beats
While I become known as a heavenly soulful chap, maybe
With the grace of God/Allah
And the Angels cheering, on and on, on my side
Whose guiding light I follow, on, on wisely
Leaving you forever, ever in my wake – Begone!

Guiding Light

Please hear my prayer; I beseech thee
Oh, Lord and Master
Hear these, my words, I do speak in all sincerity
Guide me in peaceful mindfulness
Your guiding lights shining brightly
Forever upon my soul.

I look for the wings of angels
Blessing me with streaming words, that I must write
In fulfilment of your promised destiny
As ordained by you my Lord, my Master
In pursuit of a guided peace and harmony

For all, upon this world of manifested soils.

The cycles of life, in continuance, spinning on and on
Orbiting, orbiting, around and around our little tiny glistening star
While in its turn, revolving predictably in harmonically fine-tuned influences
With the Milky Way and its centrally formed black hole
And we, my lord, my master
Cycle as do the tidal seas
In eternally fluctuating mood swings.

Please hear my prayer; I beseech thee, now
As I call upon winged angels from on high
To hear these words, I do speak in all sincerity
Allowing them as I write, to echo relentlessly throughout far, far, off reaches of the globe
To sow a single seed of heavenly wisdom
To grow, blossom and bloom in a child's untainted mind
Who'll bring joy, peace, and a little harmony, to your created Garden of Eden.

No More, No More

No more, no more, I beg you, no more
I'll give, and I'll give until I drop, but
No more, no more, I know not which
My heart in one place, my soul in another.

What is this, delusional reality?
On the one hand, frightful, vengeful, power-hungry materialistic improvisations
Full of wanton desires, wishes, fears and dreams
On the other, a peaceful, blissful heavenly place.

No more, no more, I beg you, now, no more,
For my worlds are colliding, dividing, tearing me into two
Impossible, impossible, now, to live in one or the other

Until, perhaps, my symbionts separate company upon my death, leaving an empty shell resting truly in peace, as I, return to heavenly bliss.

I do not wish to die, to evade an unwanted wanton, hellish
Illusionary world, leaving loving family, friends

Clearly, in my wake, to mourn, to grieve an empty shell,
My bodily host, an once duality of differing realities.

No more, no more, I say, no more, enough is enough
I must seek to find, to resolve, my dilemma, this disparity
Or sufferance will be the consequences for this, my life, upon the planes of Hades
I must seek, therefore, to diminish, to quell, these demonic thoughts, feelings and emotional indifference.

I sit in calm serenity, my thoughts turning inward, inward, to seek there the kingdom of my heaven
Deeper, deeper into the depths of a once familiarity
Letting go, letting go of my worldly self, acknowledging only, in simplicity
Coming home, unveiling my true nature, my part of everything – my God/Allah within!

My Lord, I Beseech Thee Now!

My Lord, my Master
I am but your humble servant
A human, a mortal being
A man, of blood, flesh, tears and bone
Born of women and will always be such.

I see, I see, am aware, all too aware
Of the suffering, the plight of so, so many, many
Who suffers, who weep in their silence, in pain and alone.
I beg you now, beg you, I beseech thee to hear my prayers
For guidance in these matters, now.

Please help me, my Lord, please help me
To shed these mortal characteristics and emotional tendencies
My desire, fears, anxieties, wishes, dreams and the need to fulfil
My sole purpose, here upon earth, as a man
To fornicate, to reproduce, to nurture, to love, the pleasures I will, will gladly forever forgo.

Please, please, I humble myself upon the ground before you
To help me let go, let go, let go
Of these earthly shackles, tying, binding me, my hands
To see, to hear, to sense, to smell, to touch, as you in your heavenly wisdom
To comprehend, the suffering, the hopeless demonic infestations, torturing, plaguing this earthly plane.

Help me, Lord, my Master in thy loving wisdom and compassion
To do something, just a little something, anything
To help my fellow humans, free themselves
Of their shackles, the locks, the chains forever binding them to suffer in vain.
And to free them from their sufferings, now and forever…

Are You Lost?

Are you lost?
In a world
Full of people
And yet, alone
Despairing
Fearful for your mind
Your soul
Then fear not
For I am with you
For I, too, have been
Into these wretched places

And crevasses of my mind
Nowhere to run
Nowhere to hide.

There is a light
Burning bright
A forever guiding hand
Believe me not
It is there
And, so am I!

"Social and Miscellaneous"

Farewell

It's now so obvious to me
Remembering back to that
Warm, romantic, idyllic evening as we said our farewells
A June moonlit night, if I recall.
The evening spent, entwined, wrapped cosily
In one another's arms, locked together, in fevered moments
Of heaving entwining embraces, so tender, so loving
While declaring our love and our sacred vows.

Strolling, arm in arm, towards your home
Slowly, slowing, along the winding, dusty lane
Fallen leaves rustling beneath our feet, under the moonlit canopies
And shelter of the *Magnifique* elm trees.
A kiss or two upon your sweetened lips
Watching, helplessly subdued as you walked, walked away
I see you there, there amongst the shimmering moonbeams
Dimly lighting your beguiling silhouetted, ghostly figure.

I hear your whimperings, attempts to silence your distressing sobs
Drifting towards me in shadowy waves, floating upon the nightly breeze
As you walked, hesitantly, restrained, but with poise and dignity
Further, further, away, way, out of reach, of my loving arms
With an eloquence, that I may never, ever hope to see again
Or a face, so beautiful as yours, as yours, my love

A lifetime, a treasure, moment, and yet a fading memory
Uniquely, heartfelt, and stunningly imaginable.

I couldn't bear to listen, to hear your tears, rolling, rolling
One by one, down, down, your fairest cheeks
As my eyes spared me not, shedding a tear or two
While my, my face quivered, uncontrollably.
Oh, did I wish, I could run, run to you
Hold you tenderly, in my loving arms, to cuddle you once more
To whisper in your ears, sweet nothings, to tell you
I'll love you, love you, eternally.

Day followed night, swiftly, by and by
As I answered to those, I serve
A surreal moment, a realisation, a heart-retching, sickly dawning
My time to man up, dig deep, deeper than ever before, to be brave
My duty ahead, the whistle blows, echoing, echoing across barren no man's land
Over the top, over the top boys, shouts the order, after you go, laddie,
Not a chance in hell, mowed-down like skittles, hard to breathe, can't breathe
Gasping, gasping, to catch, one single breath; and one last memorised glimpse of you
Lying there, beside a lone red poppy, in blood-soaked mud, in Flander's fields.

I Walk Alone Today

I walk alone today
My mother, my sister sick
My feet already blistered, red raw
Sore to the touch, to the ground
Beneath my feet
Leaving a visibly, detectable scented trail

For prowling, predatory wild animals to follow.

Not a question of whether, or not to
No choice do I have, but to walk
A journey of vital importance
That'll fill my mind
With all mannerisms of imaginings
Whilst alone, afraid, and sometimes, terrified
Alone in the dark, dark, cold, bitter, gloomy nights.

I walk for miles and miles, and miles
Across dusty, gravelly desert, deserted trails
To fetch the daily water
That I'll carry back, balanced precariously
Thereupon my head, while it swirls
Around and around with the water
Perceptibly there upon my head.

This is the only life I've ever known
Or probably ever will
Though I spend much time, time, walking
Not a murmurous utterance of discontent
Will I show, while doing my bonded duty?
Most honourably fulfilled, collecting precious
Daily water for my tribal village families.

Laugh Though It Hurts

I have always had
A ridiculously, silly sense
Of humour, that may have
Rattled an odd few cages
Now and again.

A good run it's been
I am sure of that
Thanks to all of you
My good, true, and loyal friends

I'll always think of you.
While bouncing along
Upon my bum
Down the rough stony, hilly trails
Upon life's journeys
Cheerfully, cheerfully, as I go.

I crawled upon grazed, bleeding hands and knees
Up the twisty, windy slopes, puffing and panting as I go
What fun this is, though I do not know
It feels like
I might be having a baby.

Oh, what a dusty old and bendy, soulful trail
Big rocks and boulders to play upon
Oh, do they hurt, my poor old bum
As I twist and turn to avoid
Such fun.

Whoops! That was a big on'.
And another
Missed that one, ouch
Ouch! I am red, black, and blue
All over, I am, I am.

My journey's destination, now insight
A mile to go before I wake
I'll miss the bumps
And all of you
Goodbye, goodbye – adieu to you!

Manipulators

I'm just a poor sinner
Maybe, just like you
I will not judge you
If you do not judge me.

All learning as children
Once possessing an uncontaminated mind
Reflecting reactions of adults
Realising not what they do.

Knowing which heartstring to tug upon
While seeking parental, affectionate embraces
Though given, perhaps, a disconcerting glaze
To misbehaviours, manipulative modes.

Manipulators from early ages
Why should this be?
We're born to this world
A pure, symbiotic human host.

Once, one of those children
Learning from experts, who guided me true
Though they may never have known it
Their primogenitors meaningfully taught them, too!

Quietly in the Rain

A child sings, laughs and plays
In the gently falling rain
Floating, down, down from the cloudy skies
Another child walks, walks there in the rain
And yet, another sits there all alone
It was a child, all forlorn, quietly sobbing, sobbing in the rain.

A message sent to a healthcare worker in a far, far off distant place, to come as fast as she can
To our little thatched hut, in a village many miles, miles away
Receiving our message quite quickly, a healthcare worker came
Oh, oh, so, sadly, she arrived, arrived, just a little too, too late.

They carried out my mother, all bound and wrapped in an old dirty sheet
I no longer felt like singing, laughing, or playing, all alone in the rain
While the rain made little puddles, puddles, all around, round me
I no longer wished to walk and jump in them, making big splashes to make my mother laugh and smile
I just sat there helplessly ridged, quietly crying, crying, tears rolling down, down, my checks, as I said goodbye, goodbye, to my mother, all alone, sobbing there in the rain.

I looked, as she is carried past me, as I sat drenched, alone in the wet sodden mud
Quietly weeping, weeping, lost, afraid, angry, and so, so lonely now, for I shall never see her, see her, again
For she's going to play with the angels, angels now, instead of playing with me, above us in the skies
And for the sake of few measly tiny little blue pills, thrown away in their thousands, thousands, in the west
But never, ever, sent freely to us, even in today's age of miracles
With all, it's billions and billions of dollars, wondrous technologies, and humanitarian aid!

Splintered

I am but a weak, humble human
Wearing two hats, mindfully walking, walking, along life's ever-winding rocky road
One representing materialistic perplexities
The other, spirituality.
A man, of all season, you're forgiven for thinking
Adrift, blowing steadily in the winds of time
Bending agilely as the swaying, forever fateful Willow tree
Whist suffering devastation in insistent, deviating, prevailing storms.

I search, I seek, to rediscover, truthful, heartfelt words
Raining down, down upon us, always, a follower of many, many, religions, and philosophies
Endeavouring to embrace all emanating heartfelt, heavenly words
Drifting, in and out, from my unfettered, unenlightened mind.
I am but a humble human being
With a dream of love, purity, and compassion, for all
Open-hearted, as are my arms, to fulfil one last vision of hope
Bringing passion, peace, and harmony to all, irrespective of colour, race, religion, or creed.

To a war-torn world, pillaged, and splintered
With nothing, nothing, replacing the misery and sufferances
Of tiny crying, tearful children, weeping, weeping mothers, and fathers, all forlorn
In a world preoccupied, gullible, unsuspecting the incoming tidal waves.
A world on the very brink, the edge, though undeniably lacking urgency, disconcerting, to say the least
As bacterium, virus's mutating resilience, petty power struggles and raw resources depleting exponentially
Why are we, in a mighty hurry, marching obliviously, on and on, right over, over the edge of realism?
Instead, standing back, looking, learning, working all together, to save humanity!

Still

It's not, the cold, cold
That made her freeze
Siting fixed, motionless there, there
Crying all alone, lone
In the blackness
Of night.

Overhead firework explodes
Flashes, bangs, and wallops
That light up the skies
Colourful, bright
And oh, so, so noisy
Scary for her.

How still she is
Sitting there
All alone in the dark
Depths of night
As the fireworks
Come closer, closer.

She shakes, shakes
So frightened, frightened
Tracer fireflies
Overhead, explosions all around
And her mother, her brothers
Lay there, there beside her, bloodied, dead.

Seven years old, tiny, afraid, all alone
No one to cuddle her
No one to give a damn
No one to love her, love her
No one to care for her, now all alone
Will, will she, she, be here, tomorrow?

Suffer the Children

I always knew of all
Who suffered and suffered in silence
While trying helplessly to help
Themselves, to a better
Happier, more fruitful life.
Reinforced, so callously by many
Unmistakable, undeniable cries
Amongst the thousands and thousands

Of personal pages and profiles
In Social Media today.
Women struggling, courageously, on and on, doing battle
Day after day, after day, toiling, grafting in tears, to rear their fatherless children
In such depth of inexcusable turmoil
Underfed, impoverished souls, starving, groping, groping
Around, around, in dirty, germ-ridden rubbish for just a crust
Little, tiny fingers, filthy, never washed
No one to care, no one to help
No one to hear, hear their silent screams or tears
Falling, falling to the ground, ground, unnoticed
Unnoticed, unheard, unseen cries, desperate, disparaging cries for help.

While single mothers in far, far off lands
Despair, in desperation, beg, yes beg
For a kind-hearted man to rescue and to take them away
While other, inscrutable unmentionables take advantage, harvesting, squeezing
Any shameful reward from any vulnerable soul.
How my heart weeps, cries for them, yes, all of them
For its not just circumstances befallen all of them
But the confusion, and erratic behaviour of the hell
That is the only demonic plague, infesting humankind
And the unworthiness and shamefulness of humanity.

How lost are we, in our human development?
Our souls, true learning ground
A school for our soulful, spiritual salvation
To nullify karmically altering changes and to find that eternal peace
But how my heart weeps as the blood, sweat and tears
Is squeeze and squeezed, forever, through the eye of an hourglass
While all but a few look on in pitiful pretence, turning their gazes away

Not my problem, they explicitly utter under their breath, in an untemptable show
Of ignorance, for we are, all human after all, and not to help a distressed person
Is undeniable, despicable, and indeed, an aberrant disgraceful inhuman act.

Time to Wake Up

Wake up, wake up
Time to wake up, to face reality
Humanity is languishing
In its own, inherited indulgences.

Costs too high, too many, many, innocents festering
Lonely cries, dreamers weeping, weeping, unnecessary, necessary sufferance
Mixed-up feelings, befuddled emotions, no one to turn to, nowhere to run, to hide
A world of suffering hindrances saliently.

Populations unbalanced
Animals wavering upon extinction
Raw resources used disparagingly
Too ignorant, foolish behaviours of humanity.

Prideful, confrontational to the bitter, end
No, give nor take, no turning cheek
No rendering, just a little, to enrich life or feeling
Existent upon the manifested plane reality.

Our half of dichotomy, of the duality of symbiosis
Perceptions of grandeur and deluded infectious realities
Of all, supposedly loved, though many, many, observed, shameful, destructions and desecrations
Rejecting underhandedly, the harmonising – oneness of all.

Warm and Cosy, Are We?

How it pours, ever dripping, dripping
Down, down our window panes
Making puddles for children to jump and play
And streams in gullies upon the ground
And on down, down the road to venture forth
The quickest way to the sea, to the sea.
How it sometimes floods across the plains
Giving life to unexpected dormant seeds
Carried perhaps, not lovingly upon the winds
That forever blows in gusts and waves
Intermittently taking its time and fancy, maybe
For the rain is there but never the wind, to dry your laundry.

How often has it crossed your mind?
To think or even consider
The plight of those poor wretched souls
While you are all tucked up warm
And cosily in your warm, centrally heated homes
beds and even cars.
While there are sick animals right there, right there
Next to your home, although you never thought to or cared
To look and wonder, just what might have been
If you had only looked, though couldn't be bothered
To either think or get up to look, or both maybe
Leaving the sick creature there to die, to suffer alone in pain.

But what if it hadn't been a deserved animal or bird
Would that make a difference, now to you?
What if it had been a child, crying, dying there alone in
pain?
Tummy empty, extended, bloated, full of worms and much,
much worse
Would that make a difference now, or is it enough, to blindly
look, but never to see?
You may have missed this poor, orphaned, homeless child
Whimpering not, for lifeless, its body be

Left all alone on a cold, dark, fearful, screaming, howling night
While you sit cosy and warm in your centrally heated home
While the reality is, that there are many, many poor helpless souls out there, begging, screaming, crying out in suffering pain, just for your help
But what frightens me most of all, is what is more – you know it!
So, what are you, yes you, going to do, now? Dig deeper?

The Middle Road

Please walk the middle road with me
And let us share the load
Through river valleys to their estuaries
Forests, green and city alleys
Mindfully as we walk.

Others will take the higher road
Diminishing oxygen will make them ill
Others the lower rocky trails
Fallen rocks and boulders here
Will surely, make walking extremely difficult.

Life is very much like this
One to tread most carefully
The higher road most challenging
While falling fowl of extremes
The other quite the opposite.

May I humbly suggest, most respectfully
The middle road
Is the one true and only road
To see you safely home again
With your wondrous load, safely intact.

Water Please!

Please, please help me count
The poor and the needy
Lost and forgotten souls, fallen, deep, deep
Into the caresses of their very own minds.

Crying there forlornly, helpless and alone
No tear to shed, dry empty eyes
Where once there were streams
A sponge, wrung to its limits, empty air pockets remain.

So, many, many consumed and countless, drained, and fatigued
Scratching a living from sun-baked, dust-ridden soil
No water to speak of, for drinking or watering the crops
For it's miles and miles to the nearest watering hole.

A container humped upon one's shoulders like a bag of black sooty coal
Or upon one's heads, whichever one prefers
A long, long way to labour, to drag it so far, far, back home
For a sip of worm-infested, dirty water, to quench one's thirst.

My arms, my legs shaking, exhaustingly, in unstoppable
Movements, though I try very hard not to show it, or my fatigue
Nor my exhaustion to my dependant loved ones, for fear they'll break down and cry
And not let me go tomorrow, a slave to the realities, of my life.

Cannot they dig a well, next to our village
For all the village people to share as one big family
Together, now, and forever with blessings from above
To have clean water would be a little miracle, it'll be.

We Are the Unworthy

I walk along my predestined journey through life
Ordained, with true wisdom and forethought of mind,
karmically, systematical, natural,
By the good grace of the holy, truly, and all-knowing, all-seeing
Almighty, who sits not in judgement
Upon our deeds, but watches, diligently o'er us
Lending his guiding hand, where needs be
Sending his guardian angels to shine
A beacon upon our wayward, misguided paths.

Though it sends shivers, through and through, racing up and down my spine
In the knowledge that we
The manifested populous, keepers of the garden
The created playground, sown, nurtured for us, by God/Allah's almighty hands
Are not, not, worthy mangers of all we survey
For we are deceitful, despicable, thieving retches
Tyrants and manipulators, dancing not to the harmonies
Sacrosanct tunes of the Almighty, but to our own unsavoury devious, ineptitude soulless songs.

No better time to change, no better time to encompass, to embrace
The true values and wisdom of the heavens
No more intrinsically woven webs or entangled entwined apple trees
Pursuing ill-conceived, contrived, concocted
Singular moments of lightning accelerated, insignificant moments of happiness, gone, gone in a flash
Devil be gone, gone, out the heads of children
The children of the world, of enduring sufferance
The children of our creator, the all-seeing, sage, all-knowing, all-seeing – Omnipotent One!

Why?

There's no doubt that we're all human
Hell-bent on defending extremely honourable beliefs,
Our religion, way of life,
And maybe our philosophical ideologies, too.
It appears to be an inbuilt trait or peculiarity, to defend, to act
And react, to one another's beliefs
In a manner befitting a buffoon, while, by our very own nature, we're literally
Destroying, that which we devotedly believe.

Every religion or philosophy I've ever studied or known
Scribed, somewhere within its, holy or not, scriptures
Passed down by the prophets of old; that we should
Love one another, as if, we were, brothers, or sisters.
Yet here we are, all, hell-bent for leather
Upon destroying, the very fabric, essences, and foundations
Of those holy scriptures, defending words, we truly believe in
While ironically desecrating and extinguishing everyone.

When the truth of the matter is surely
With one truly omnipotent creator – God/Allah!
Who created every one of us?
To whom we all individually pray, irrespective of religious denominations or philosophical beliefs.
Making a mockery of everything we stand for and believe in,
While surrendering to subtly inferred and persuasive impulses
Becoming a servant to the devil incarnates
Egotistical minds, demonic desires, wishes and dreams.

Untethered Love

Hear the world sing for us
Echoing, chants of love, of passionate joys
Ceaseless caressing waves, upon the warming heartfelt
breezes
Embracing lover, everywhere.

Listen to the birds on high
Joyous blessings, beneath comforting clouded skies
Heartfelt pleasures of enlightening spring
Life's renewing energies.

I will kiss you upon the lips
Tenderly touching, a delicate little butterfly
Fluttering upon the gentle wind
Confetti glistening, raining down.

Love eternally shining, elations, just for us
Forever ever and a day, it'll be
Growing stronger, stronger with every sweetened embrace
Untethered, all-encompassing – love!

“Spiritual”

A New Age Dawning

The time is almost nigh
When change and time
Will once again, anoint the heavens
When angels descend, from on high
To grace us with their loving presence
Guiding lights and beacons, shining ever brighter
Than ever was, lighting the path we do tread
To the true reality, bringing heavenly peace upon the earth.

Even though the world’s in constant flux
New insightfulness will be dawning
As the sun bows down, humbly unveiling
The unimaginable, to all those who seeketh
The heavenly peace, unbound, untethered
Within their very, very own shells;
Why, therefore, live to endure, forever in the shadows
The humdrum existence of an illusionary materialistic world.

Complete with all its sufferance, for every single soul
Who suffers, many hardships, in one illusionary form or another;
Only you, you, can unlock your delusionary imaginings
To uncloak the true reality, that is there for the asking
To all those who seeketh, with honour and true devotional wisdom
So, so rare, rare, today, while the world unfolds slowly
In its beleaguered way, leaving us to change our futures

Having the will, ability, and emotive endurance.

We cannot change the world's impermanence, for time and space rolls on
But adjust its illusionary perceptions upon our bodies habitually controlling minds;
Let us, therefore, all strive together, as one united people, to eradicate all the sufferance, whoever walked the earth
With all due endeavours, to seek, to find and veil the true reality
In realisations of many changing moments, like a cinema film playing, frame by frame
Altering our perceptions, of time, space, and our delusionary notations
Uncloaking the true heavenly and peaceful reality, within
To the bewilderment of our egos, controlling influences.

All Unique

To dream, to dream
Dreams becoming the master
Conniving, fiendish imaginings
Incessantly rumbling, twisted perceptions
Influences, subtly, stealthily invading
Prevailing, beyond the realms of realism
Control of one's ineffective abilities.

Every individual, unique unto themselves
A mutation of the true omnipotent ones
Almighty hands, though not of the present
Or the moment of conception
Hosts open door, inviting essences, our souls
To become one, with inconceivable realities upon the manifestation
Microcosmically created, orgasmic world paradise, earth.

All different, evolutionary mutants of a long-forgotten seed
Influences of many, life's experiences for one

Millions of permutations of resiliencies, imperceptibility.
Chemical indifferences from one to another, running deeply, through one's veins
While genetics run rampant, making us uniquely different
Snuggling up to karmically adjusting environmental influences
Acting upon singular, dualities, symbiont within!

Are We an Illusion?

I look to the east and the west
I look to the north and the south
And even look up and down
What do I see, I see the stars?
One life, this life; one moment, this moment
One goal, one reality
Your time to choose, right now.

You're not quite as fit or as motivated as an athlete
Or, trained and prepared as the toughest fighters on earth
Physical limits, far, far, away from those of your far-reaching imaginings
But the gift you possess, a precious, wondrous gift.
Intellectual abilities, please, please, don't waste them
Or the reason for your existence, the gift of life
A purpose of fulfilling, a destiny to seek, to harmonise, to become one with the emptiness of the nothingness, beyond time, beyond space, and the manifestations that are the dualities of heaven and earth.

I oft' rest there in peaceful harmonies
In a place where reflections, neither come nor go
No echoes heard from the manifested plane, no senses of a humankind
My mind as one, deep, deep, within itself.
The spirit has no gender, no vulnerabilities, or weaknesses
But to inhabit its symbiotic host, dwelling incognito, learning, to absorb, to grow

To watch, to conquer, the extremes and cunning follies, the demands of the egotistical mind.

I look in all directions, seeing nothing, nothing but the stars and stars, in a delusional universe
While oft' the silent many, ask the reason, why
And in my heart of heart, I know reality is an emptiness
The world, never here, nor you and I, as the world is an illusion
A mass of vibrating particles spinning around and around in vast empty spaces
A vision never, ever seen of an illusion, to the deluded mind's naked eye
And the manifested opposite of the unmanifested collective, the dualities that are, heaven and earth.

Astral Body

Every night in the dark depths of night, while my ego
Sleeps, dreaming, dreaming, the night and its cares away
Unaware my soul is in ascendance
Leaving, leaving, rising, rising from
Its vessel, its symbiont, the body, my vessel
Departing for a while, to revitalise, bathing in the ever-flowing
Cosmic energies of the unmanifested plains.

Floating free, free as a bird
Just above, above its host, hosts bodies
Joined together, tethered
Chained, shackled in bondage
By a silvery twisting cord, no different
To the human mother, child
Umbilical cord.

A bond so, so strong
Relaxation of the host, a key factor to the needs of the Spirits
Rise in ascendance, as electrically charged energy

Binding symbionts adhesively together
A robust and worthy bond of loving cooperation
To break, to be, separated
Institutively by the astral body.

A peaceful natural phenomenon, nothing to fear, to worry about, unnecessarily
Though it is a near-death experience without
The traumatic event that oft' precede its flight
While death comes to us all, at some point or another
It is only, only when the silvery cord has severed
Our journeys ended in our bodies, returning to dust
And the essence of our souls remaining, to the unmanifested plains, repeatedly recycling, until enlightenment prevails.

Balanced Moderations

Life is meant, for living, our teacher within
Balancing moderations
The middle road of mindfulness
Loving, peaceful harmonies.
Doses of tempered excitement
Lots of love and compassionate tenderness
Permeating waves of warming, purposeful, loving, eternal rays of radiating energies
Shimmering, gleeful colourful auras, seen by few.

Place your feet, cautiously
Not to step on a flee
Walking, there in front of you
Tiny, unnoticeable, camouflaged by size.
While always remembering, thou, you're walking alone
Upon the Middle Road to freedom
There are many, many, others walking with you
Thou, many, many, thousands of differing time zones.

Thoughts, feelings, and emotions, along the way
Desires and dreams are acceptable, kind, heartfelt pleasures

While not becoming a slave to them
A definitive, mindful prerequisite.
Helping one another, fulfilments of dreams
Honourable timely fashion
Will count as good karma
Cycling lifetimes, upon illusionary manifested planes.

Be Still, to Learn

Still, yourself, sit a while
Learning patience, tolerance and understanding
Towards inner demons, your very own chattering
Flowing perpetually within the emptiness of infinity.
Disturbing, external forces
Light and sound waves, flowing in
Filtering, through and through, one's windowpane
Shimmering shadows upon the ground.

Too fast, for eyes perceptions of intermittency
Bouncing, reflections off of me
Deflecting waves of auric energy
Radiating outward, loving transparencies.
Flowing freely through the symbiotic host
Awakening coiled serpent resting in calming serenity
Rising with every breath, I take
Gently opening invisible spiritual conduits within.

Astral body floating free, released from bondage
Ascending up, up, to cosmic oceanic seas
Venturing forth, my heart's desires
Into vast emptiness, realisations, abiding oneness, with all.
Time stands still, or seemingly
Time one singular moment, now
Jelled, interdependent upon the manifested plane
Harmonising with circling sun, moon, and Galaxy.

Beneath the Spoken Words

It's not the words, not the words
Written down, black, white, all colours of the rainbow
Marks upon paper
Upon a digital screen, an electronic book, maybe.

It's not the ancient texts or manuscripts
Scribed, transcribed, and translated
Modified, to suit the purposes of the few, maybe
For the desires of those seeking power over their minions.

How many can read and memorise
To quote, chapter and verse by heart
And yet, how many truly understand
The deeper meanings, truly spoken, hidden beneath the writings.

Words, never written, but etched into the hearts and souls of humanity, though no words were ever spoken
Inspirational, silently spoken and transcribed in magnifico depth of feeling, rare
Of heart, love, and compassion and earnest honesty
Of a truly intrinsically translucence, valued above, beyond.

These are the true riches, riches, true wealth
Woven with eloquence, threaded, unseen, into, and in amongst the written word
Such feeling, such passion and yet, few, few
Rarely delve, deep, deep into the depths of their own, inner sanctums
To understanding all who risked life and limb, to speak, bringing forth, glorified heavenly scented woods.

Blindly Following

I will not follow blindly
Like a lamb
Driven-to-the-slaughter
To gaze helplessly
Upon the demise of all humanity.

We follow all too readily, the paths of sheep
In blind disregarding of obedience
Of the teaching of the ancient
Prophets of old.

And yet, we were, given
An assumed intelligence
By the good grace of God/Allah
To use wisely, in his absence.

While we shamefully claim deniability
While indulging in such profanities
And creations of ours, our egotistical mind
Allowing it unprecedented reign o'er our minds.

Without having a consequentiality and feasibility
Of a realistic and permanent solution
To save us from annihilation
And the death of yet, another civilisation.

We must all walk the road of mindfulness
Walking the path of righteousness
In seeking the truth, love, and compassion
And to the peace within!

Bow to the Wind

I bow down, down, upon my knees
Surviving the mighty winds, unforgiving temperamentalities
Ceaselessly streaming across, clouded skies.

I am lucky, agile, flexible; I am, Willow
Curtsying to gusting, ever-flowing, incessant airstreams
Uplifting, spirited, lower-lying shrubbery, heathers, and green grasses
Clinging, clinging, in despair, to bare, rugged landscapes.

Possessing natural mutability
Yielding effortlessly to buffeting gales
Green bark coverings, resisting, swirling, battering whimsicalities.
Though jealous of one's athleticism and freedoms, for deep-rooted, fixed,
Pinned to grounded, am I
No escaping, or liberating movement to commute, have I
My irreversible destiny awaits.

Your journey necessary, deep-seated, karma adjusting
Though deep-rooted, you've choices, for now
Unlike mine, stuck in the mud, a duration, a lifetime
Embark now, upon your destiny's journey.
Letting resistances fade terminally, resilience a necessity, always submissive to air currents
Seek ye first, controlling interest o'er your heart, mind, body, and soul
Winds of times, a changing, blowing – onward, onward, for now.

Acclimatising to change, or suffering inexorable consequences, from time-honoured
Servants, karma influencing airstreams
Submissive reflection, calming, guiding; not a whisper, a hint
Not a hair's breadth of immunity, let go, let go
Subtle subservience, a softened elegance, feeling sensed
One's shallow, flawlessly flowing breath, calmly exhaling, inhaling, in and out
Involuntarily, oxygenating body, mind, and soul

Embracing incoming waves, of time, space, and illusionary realities.

Bowing down, down, careful to the mighty winds of change
A snail's pace, unveiling peace, harmony, and the nothingness of all
Returning the manifested planes to evolutionary paths
Devoted millions, taking opportunistic control over influential destines
Glimmerings of hope, along the way, to a soulful, peaceful, relaxing place
Truly amazing, perceptual, heavenly blissfulness
Enlightenment, perhaps!

Calling Whispers

Hear them calling in their silences
Day and night, echoing tormented whispers
Lingering ceaselessly, blowing in and in
Upon cosmic waves of oscillating energies.

Few hear them, calling them to school
Few devotees, in mindfulness, sit to listen
In patient silences, of the mind
Rattling cages, unlocking chains.

Faded whispers from on far
Barely audible, wavy messages, translucency
Ancient voices, raining down
Undulations copiously ignored, except for the few.

Resonating ambiances flowing in
Meandering streams, silent murmurings
Whispering teachings, wise and true
Falling disgracefully upon deaf, uncaring muted ears – yours!

Casting Shadows

Glistening sunrays shining
Through and through, one's window panes
Casting shadows upon the walls
Cloudy shimmerings upon the floor
Feathers crossing empty spatial dependency.

Stuff that dreamers, romanticise about in droves
Flights of fancy, all the rage
Quivering there, beneath one's own feet
Mindfulness to be adhered to, with each step
Disturbing the natural eloquences.

Please, please, don't cast a shadow, or doubt
O'er one's new and unexpected, joy
Casting undeviating shadows o'er us
Closing doors upon one's soul
Barricading glimmering hopes, and shadowy dancers
gracefully prancing across one's floor.

Choose?

You are one of those
Are you not?
Sitting upright and proud
In your warm, comfy armchair
At home, who sits and stares
Only to turn your head
In a thought-provoking bonanza.
Your dreams at night
As you quietly sleep in your comfy bed
Of the precious gifts, a diamond maybe
To receive, to have or to give
In a mindless extravagant mist
Of triviality while other, others.

Poor wretched souls, struggle oft' to lift their heads'
To watch, to stare, in stunned expressionless silences
For they're the poor, the mild, the meek, suffering, suffering
Frequenting our street and just maybe, sleep in dosshouses
Whose lives are so simple, laying quietly in the gutters, helplessly
While yours is one of a luxurious pretence.
Blinkered to all but to possess a pressurised, heated, piece of hardened carbon
The diamond you'll be wearing upon your finger or around your neck
Gracing you with just a flickering, fleeting moment of happiness
When they're starving, begging, yes begging for a simple morsel
A scrap of bread, a little piece of fruit
To sustain them, sustain them, through a bitterly cold, long night.

Of course, they're your choices to make
Whether or not to respond and ask how high
To jump to the excessive continuous demands
Upon your naivety, while trying so desperately
To fulfil the unreachable joys and happiness
In this world, but demanded by your demonic egotistical self.
Real blissful joys and happiness are miraculous pleasures
Granted to those who seek, to find, to understand
True peace, pure bliss comes forth, from deep, deep within
As the eradication of the controlling freak, the egoic mind progresses
Whose demands are how high you chose to jump
Rather than forgoing and deciding to give, just a tiny wee treasured morsel.

Come on. Come on!

Come on, come on, what is it with us?
All born from out of God/Allah? Almighty hands
Are we starved of intellectual abilities, perhaps?
Has the distance from our eyes to the end of our noses grown exponentially as piccolo's
Are we so self-absorbed, with our egotistical wishes and desires?
With its ceaselessly flowing illusionary imperceptive agendas
Narcissistic capricious, illusionary self-serving irrationalities
And promises of blissful, euphoric feeling of joy, but only giving, giving ever, unfulfilled, unsatisfactory endings instead.

Stuck firmly are we, in a muddy quagmire, no true realistic sensibilities, or even a conceptual, concrete value of what is true bliss
Just cravings, stretching elasticity with no sited end
Rushing around as if there is no tomorrow.
Is it so, so, imperative to seek, treasures and riches?
Of the materialistic world for self-gratifications
While robbing, pillaging, and raping the left resources
We treasure now
But will our great, great-grandchildren in a hundred, two hundred years from now – I wonder?

Do we need to push boundaries further and further?
Out and out, beyond the realms of humans, insanities and into the coals of Hades
Creatively flaunting, waving, righteous integrity into the faces of the many, for the sake of a fistful of dollars
And how? Entrapment, maybe, legal bud
Trapping unsuspecting naïve wonderful country folk with more trickery than in a magician's box
Paraphernalia and complexities, whilst preying upon their habitual acceptance, trust, and complacencies

Are we in a hurry? Calm down, calm down, relax, it isn't a
race, with a hostile ending, or is it?
Rushing around as if the earth is exploding and on fire, fire –
Why?

Are You Comfortable in Silence?

Are you comfortable?
In the silence, silence, silence
Feelings of in trepidations
Flowing through and through, your head.
Uneasy, apparent sensitivities
Afraid and apprehensive of being alone, alone
Deprived of all thoughts, feelings, or emotions
Senses cling onto, uncomfortable simplicities.

Awareness of senses heightened?
Mind confused and bewildered, whilst,
Fearing countless, inexplicable anxieties, running, running,
streams.
Screaming out, watcher, watcher, beware!
What does this all amount to?
What does this all, truly mean?
Why not try a little experiment to see?
Perceptions of reality, static, motionless, inside your head.

A darkened room is what you'll need
Dusk having come and gone
Eliminating all proactive internal complexities
Outside impediments and influences, a bare minimum
The experiment has begun.
Unknown realms of imperceptibility dominate
Shadowy depths, the abyss, awareness of the void.
The truly remarkable, oneness of self-seen!

Constantly Wishing

You're one of those, foolish dreamers
Constantly wishing, wishing
Your life away, away, and away
For fleeting, uninspiring moments of happiness
Vanishing whiffs of smoke in the wind
Faster than ever conceived.

Dreams and desires, you're trailing
Here in the moment, a moment
Though soonest, gone, gone, gone
One-dimensional rushes of chemical reactivities
Self-gratifications, vaporising
Leaving you, stranded, alone and in all, a little bit deflated
Perplexed, forgotten, in wonderment, as to where sensual feelings have dissipated, too.

What is it, with all you humans?
There is much to be learnt and to do
In the manifested
When there're many, many moments
Betwixt, the then, and the now
To savour, to live, to enjoy
In mindfulness and contemplative pursuits.

Pure bliss doesn't come easily
For one, who's forever chasing rainbows
Illusive, supposed, magical treasured gold
Though it does occur, with the purest of love and compassion
Radiating, out, and out, and out
Felt, seen, and sensed, introspectively, while
Seeking, unveiling oneness, in true blissfulness within.

Death!

Let us consider one, solitary, inconsequential word
The word *"Death"*.
For many a frightening, blood-curdling, nightmarish,
fiendish word
Screaming, terminal, though never is
Your essence of soul, returns to the cosmic sea, karma
controlling
The unmanifested collective plane, unless…???

An experiment, I know, due right now
Attestation for doubters everywhere
Of the ephemerality transitory nature of moments of now
Strung together, a movie, no less
A lifetime of individualities
Millions of illusionary frames.

Idolatry is a prerequisite, one of many paths
I bid thee, now, to walk hand in hand, with me
To leave your physical, empty shell
Guided consciousness, an internal, interstellar compass
Flying free upon the cosmic, oceanic, esoteric waves
Awareness, individualistic, free spirit.

It may happen immediately or take many moons
Lay flat on your back, calming all thoughts
Relaxing the body, as if preparing for sleep
Transferring energies, to one singular, focused point
While struggling to free, the soul from its symbiotic host
Falling asleep, and then…?

One unsuspecting day, when all is calm, and you sound
asleep
You'll awaken, discovering a paralytic corpse
While your soul endeavours, to untethering itself
Tugging upon your immobilised body, like removing your
finger from sticky paper

Focus, focus; let not, your mind wanders, now,
A static jolt, esoteric electricity, and you'll be flying – free!

Do You Hear Them?

I've lived in the shadows
For many a year
The shadows of my *Homo sapiens'* mind
Always seeking, always looking
Still searching, ever weary but aware,
Of the truth, the underpinning of this one true moment, of now
The true reality, the illusion that is the manifested plain.

My soul, young or old, maybe, no matter, placed here
To watch, to learn, to evaluate the tormented
Demonic tortures, torrentially flowing here
To study closely, the experiences of life confining
Of an essence, a soul, of a free-flowing norm, pure energy
Telepathically endowed, an enlightened amnesiac
Bound and tethered to a rotting, festering, smouldering earthly plain.

I hear them, do you hear them calling
The angelic trumpeter's harmonies fanfares
The thunderous welcoming, titans, clashing in the winds
The clouds parting, unveiling the shiniest, brightest, blinding beams of light, radiating down, down, upon our heads
I sense an electrifying euphoria, of statically charged energetically, free-flowing elations, of love, joy and happiness, drifting, drifting
In waves, pouring, falling, from the heavenly skies, like mystic rain.

I hear your wise, heartfelt words of guidance to humanity
A blessed beacon, showering down, down upon us, now
And influential spiritual presence, a graceful holy eloquence that is

The one true Omnipotent One, creator of all
I bow to thee upon the ground, my Lord God/Allah
I understand, descending gifts are for all, all your earthly creatures
Irrespective of form, colour, race, religion, or creed – we welcome them with arms outstretched.

Dream or Reality?

I dream, dream, I'm holding you, securely
Wrapped up, cosily in heartfelt, tender, loving arms
Above fluffed up cloudy skies, way up, up, on high
Twinkling stars and radiantly shining, smiley friendly moon.

Transmitting warming, wavy light moonbeams
Caressing, kindled, guiding starlit bright
Spirits flying faster than the speed of light
Into one's welcoming open arms.

Butterflies in a courtship dance
Graceful eloquence, delicate wings
Fluttering, swirls, twists, and turns
Poetic motions of nature harmonising, loving passions.

Making love, in spirit, not the flesh
Flying free in floods of joyous tears
Dancing nakedness, embracing
Sweetened loving movements in harmony.

Happy souls becoming one, in universal harmonies, now to part
Off to mountains, far, far off distant peaks and lands
Your perfumed flowering spreading wings
Dreaming dreams, or reality?

Embedded

An intrinsic, embedded web of intrigue
Of universal incorporating manifestations
A structural ametaphysicality
Influencing, and influenced, by natures
Karmic inherent, cycling wheels of life.

Our wishes, desires, dreams
Thoughts, feelings, and emotions
Innate, entwined and interwoven
Complexities, unknown karmic
Universal abnormalities.

An evolutionary hiccup, a malfunctioning
Anomaly in the unmanifested design
Unforeseen, unwanted, now entrenched
Into the manifested illusionary perceived realities
And spiritualistic symbiont's playground.

The human, *"I"*, has choices
Enthused guardianship and defending
Custodians of the manifested planes
Walking mindfully, bathed in calming blissful seas
Of tranquillity.

Or choose self-indulgent, self-gratifying fulfilment
Of limiting, oft' fleeting, indistinguishable, forgettable
moments
Of happiness, to the melodic marching, and unpredictable
natured
One and only, incarnation of demonic sufferance's
The evolutionary, inhumane abomination – the human
Egotistically dispensable, interfering, internal influence.

Energy of Light

Energy of light, flowing spiritually within
Permeating, through and through, one's outer rim
In shimmering waves, glowing, poetic shades of a coloured hazy glim
Out, out, from the body, the vessel, the symbiotic host
Surrounding coloured, circling rings
Around and around a puddle, upon the ground.

Changing colours as the pendulum swings
Moods fluctuating with gusting playful winds
The spirit within, the soul, the astral body
Creating circling coloured waves, of energetically flickering light
Unless you've mastered control, releasing the serpent within.

Body and soul entwined together, tethered
For a lifetime of synergy with one's symbiotic, protective host
Bestowing upon it, in perpetuity, awareness of consciousness
Regulator, over the body, the once empty shell
While spirit, learning the mysteries of life, upon illusionary manifested planes.

Essences of Soul

I am, an essence of soul
From the unmanifested collective's essences of souls
A plane within the manifested
The unobserved, mystically cloaked, imperceptibly acknowledged dark matter.

Opposite of Pauli's exclusion principle,
The unmanifested and the manifested
Illusionary perceptions of reality

Simplistically embedded, interweaving reflections.
Not being privy to scientific knowledge or jargon
My previous symbiotic host
A poet, who strung words meaningfully together
Similarly, to the symbiotic relationship, controlling light and dark matter.

There are many, many more amazing questions, than answer
Rattling around, and around, the known universe
Keeping embryonic dualities, unlike me, blindly calculating
Indifferences, betwixt relativity and quantum mechanics for instance
Two simplistic complexities embedded, within abysses of nothingness.

Evolution

Are you one to seek the pleasures?
Of a physical nature
Upon the manifested planes
Strong urges, urges to reproduce
Accelerating, day by day
An explosion of tiny beings
In the most unrealistically proportioned.

Unsustainable in an ever expandable
Changing populous, upon the world
Leaving desperate weeping, pathetic lives
Suffering in silent solitude
In pain, minds swirling, confused, deluded
Bodies twisted, shaking, gnawing, always choking
While souls demented diluted ineffectually spiritualistically.

Living the nightmarish, feverish, actual living Hell
While others wallow in luxuriance
Though many try to help intrinsically in vain
As all God/Allah's creations evolve
Evolving in an inconstant transient reality

Bodies and souls in continuous flux
Pulsating to possible exponential extremities.

Life's not for the faint-hearted upon the edge
But for those mindful in their daily devotions
Bringers of peace and harmony to the lost, to the damned
No celebrations of effigies or remembrances
Pure devotional practices while balancing the
responsibilities to the manifested plane
To the evolutionary endeavours, craving of our souls
Uniting finally, amalgamating body, symbiont, into one,
essence of soul.

Eyes of Reason

Eyes of reason
Sent to watch, to quell
All thoughts, feelings and emotive unreasoning
Twisted, unconscionable perceptions
And rationalisations.

Drifting sand dunes
Across the manifested
Illusionary, wind-swept planes
Swamping populous of deluded souls
Inclusive cohabiting symbiotic hosts.

Souls, seeking truth
Of reasons, not irrationalities
Oh, so, much already lost?
Thrown away in senseless ludicrous haste
And inexcusable disregard to truth.

Ancient, cherished, and treasured, spiritual wisdom
Gifts from free-spirited, indigenous tribes
Once thriving, across our manifested illusionary plane
Therefore, remember these words spoken, though
bittersweet, to some, lest we forget, once

We were – family!

Falling Star

I am a falling star
Flashing through, dark, darkened skies
Alone and very, very hopeful
Of what is yet to be.

I was a rising star
At least upon a Facebook page
Now, all I am is falling, falling
A falling star from heavenly grace.

Nowhere left to shine
Nowhere to go
But down, down, down through the heavens
A shooting star, I be.

I am a falling star
Burnt out and all alone
My destiny unfulfilled, one last, momentary flash
So, so bright, bright, now to die, extinguished, all, all, alone!

Fear Not!

Fear not, for life is not
What it seems
With its illusionary perceptions
Egotistical desires, wishes and dreams.
They are the devil incarnate
The only living hell, there'll ever be
Your creation, your subconscious
Raising the stakes, enriching one's soul.

No nightmares here, natural playing forces
Universality controlling karma
Influences, upon all we do, all we survey
A guiding light, conciliatorily forging one's destiny.
Mindless chattering inside one's head
Incessant meddler, instigator of all distractions
Creator of all our pathetic, whimperings
In a world rife with technology, surpassing our humanities.

A balancing act, between ego
And the essences of our synergistic selves
Watching, aware of all-natural processes
Of one's symbiotic host.
Until the day of judgment, while heavenly bound
Ascending into the unmanifested plane
Processing soul's empirical, materialistic realisations
While intuitionistic adapting karma.

Life's cycling, as the weather
Infinitely rotating cycle
Nothing here to fear
All, evolutionary occurring processes
Birth, death, assimilating valued information
Returning cycles, too, and from, the abyss, an unimaginable void
An emptiness, the unmanifested cosmic oceans
Of nothingness, blissful, peacefully harmonious.

From the Heart

It has been many, many years spent
Quietly, contemplating in a self-created, lonely exile of solitude, but not bliss
Fearful, but ever diligent, watching, learning from my very own alter-ego's habitual, ill-conceived
Fluctuating and menacing, attention-seeking, screams and impromptu imaginings

Streaming, gushing, endlessly through the shadowy mindless
frustration, my moments, moments of madding weaknesses
of mindlessness
The true demonic nature and humankind's one, and only hell
to fear, here upon this earth.

Divided we have stood, speaking in many, many tongues
No one language favoured by Allah/God
In his wisdom, his division paramount and necessary
To divide and to conquer, to grow and to learn
True toleration, truly understanding, true heartfelt
knowledge, gelling in love's honourable peace, and
harmonies within
Oneness in the emptiness, of the combined, manifested and
unmanifested plains.

Learn to put aside your petty squabblings and indifferences
Bow to the will of the Almighty, to his love
His extreme sensitive, compassionate heart
Walking forever in peaceful harmonised bliss, mindful of
thought, and all, who would surround you, here, now
By day and by night, love and cherish all, without favour
Who would come knocking upon your door in the dark
depths of night, in a new wave of loving friendships and a
truly open-hearted, spirituality?

Free

I wish to leave, but not to die
My body behind an empty shell
Free in the esoteric spiritualistic planes
Betwixt the dualities of the manifested, the unmanifested
planes.

Freely expressing the beauty, the essence of soul
Warming, free-flowing, glowing aura, spiritual energy,
rarely observed, but by a few
Pure, unadulterated, perfect, mindful consciousness

Calmly aware, drifting, freely upon waves, upon rippling
karmically unmanifested, oceanic seas.

We are intrinsically focussed, revitalising energies,
resources within.
Known as Chi, Astral body, Sukshma-sharira,
Life-force to name, but a few
Patiently waiting unveiling, its sacrosanct simplicities
Freely flowing blossoming energies, essences of souls.

Flowing Wisdom

My body changing unlike the wind
I am transforming from within
Nocuous chattering inside my mind
Diminishing, with every breath, of a kind.

Light shining, a new dawning, an awakening
Spiritual energies ascending, from deep, deep within
My heart lighter, a sensed euphoria, of wellbeing
My aura is glowing, intensifying.

Radiating loving kindheartednesses, seeping waves of
purified healing energies
Streaming out, out, miraculous, unrestricted ascendant
flowings
A seed planted, by God/Allah's, all-wise, all-knowing,
almighty benevolent hands
A flower, sap rising, petals opening, blossoming, soon to
bloom – inconspicuously!

From the Skies

Descending from the skies
Breath from the heavens
I am, pure soul
Unadulterated, conscious energy
No shape, no form, an essence of soul

Affiliated to the unmanifested collective.
I am here upon manifested soils
Planes, lacking in reality or substance
An observer, being nurtured, to learn, to ripen
Consciousness, aware fully
Watching, microscopically from within
Assigned symbiotic, human host.

I am the embodiment of love and compassion
Dwelling deep, deep, within the abyss
A human, self-absorbed
Self-centred, deviously, chattering mind
Shapeshifting, pushing, bending, and twisted into reality
Harmonisation, becoming one, with an uncomfortable skin.

I'll follow and watch over my human host
Wondering why, I am, imprisoned here
In a decaying, sickly, manifestation
Inept and imperfect as it may be
While both conforming, to a delusional reality
Chain-linked tetherings, an eternity, of enduring sufferance.

I watch, from within, while one crawls, blunders, around and around
Upon little tiny feet, on a rock hard, Stony floor
Picking oneself up, looking bemused, dusting oneself off
To foolishly starting, over, and over, again, and again
Wondering, in earnest, and compassionately.

Hidden Roads

I walk a spiritual path, alone
Enriching my journeys lonesome solitary
Confining, conniving, twisted perceptualities
In mindful stepping stones across the sands
While conceiving perceptive, soulful expressions
Within my embryonical illusionary mindfulness.

I am an island, among a sea

Of juvenile soulful archipelagos
Treading uneven, rocky hidden roads
To enlighten the body, but more the soul
Though our roads similarly, bumpy, sometimes calming, too
Dusty trails, meandering, snaking, curling mysteriously.

Never two journeys, ever the same
All unique, karmically chosen to dance
In tuneful harmonies to master's whisperings
Echoing resonations from deep within
The captive shell, the once empty vessel
Symbiotic hosts.

Our thoughts, feelings and emotions, our senses, too
Virtually the same, though not me, me
That's all alone but we, we, we
While valuing our freedoms of movement
Perceptions of truth and reality
Allude the inexperienced captive juveniles we are.

Held against our will, unknowingly, karmically sealed
A duration of heavenly smiling turns
Or the insightfulness of enlightenment
Whichever ever comes first
Eternal prisoners, confined to our symbiotic hosts
Irrespective of possessed – flexibilities.

Humanity or Bust

Out there, whilst we're sleeping
Neatly wrapped up, like parcels
Cosy and warm in our beds
Men, women, and children, blown to smithereens
All bent and twisted physically, emotionally drained and despairing
By war, famine, and criminality.

What happened to our humanity?
Will it once again surpass
Our technology, in essence
Not making a difference, either way
To preventing all unnatural slaughter
From happening, it's merely up to us!

We must grasp the nettle by the horns
Sit up, take note
And shout from the rooftops, high and low
To the politicians below and the Angel above
To stop playing with self-servicing agendas
And to use one's powers wisely, a facilitated solution, hopefully.

How many Countries spend millions?
Upon their election campaign trails
Though half will never, see the light of day
Or reap the benefit of their endeavours
Nor will the 6-year-old child
Gun down, shot, bleeding profusely and left dead.

Or staving, in a far-off land
Out of sight and maybe, out of mind
For it's what these poor souls and mites
Must surely be, for few have offered
Up to help them through their sorry
Their anguish, their torturous conditions in these inhumane times.

Come on now, come on
Let's all pull together, now
Before it's too late and our souls
Are sent to hades instead off to heaven
Shamefully left to rot
In the murky depths of hell.

Imagine This!

You're afraid?
Of truthful realities, deep, deep, within
Seeking, inner conscious realisations
Wisdom, peace, and harmonies.
Unveiling unknown, mystical, intangible, conceptual realities
Qualities yet undiscovered, unknown to all, bar a few
While one goes on, floundering, a wash
Washed up fishes, upon distant shores.

Adhering to comforting, familiarity
While egoic slaves, to its creations, anxieties, desires, wishes and dreams
Wasting cycling lifetimes, in pathetic, progressively fewer pursuits
Meanderings, prideful, incessant
Encapsulating memories, temporary boosts to self-worth.
Cool your dependencies, giving the soul a real lifeline
Look to your roots, your core foundation, your essence of soul
Exist not for an eternity, wallowing pitifully in delusionary perceptions.

Apprehensive delving deep, deep, within
So, imagine this, and believe this, now
Your spirit's released, your astral flying free
Faster than light, to deep space in the blink of an eye
The serpent within, one's propelled projectile.
There goes the moon, solar system, go, go, go
Millions, and millions of miles, your left empty shell
Alone, and awaiting your spirits return
Don't think, now, don't feel, look back, back, is that you – oh, so small
Insignificant, tiny, afraid are we now – of your very own soul?

Intuitive Wisdom

Listen, listen to the intent, the meaning
Unspoken, unheard, hidden words
Following advice, often freely surrendered
Open up your heart, your mind, your psyche
Though, you may know better
Are you truly, truly, realistically sure?

Kind-hearted gestures offered
Flowing generosity from one's heart, one's spiritual essence
Respect the heartfelt impromptu gift, with graciousness
Equality of spirit as kindly tendered, embracing it
With one's open heart, mind, and psyche
Evaluating in zestful enthusiasms.

You'll never know, unless, you've listened
Possible ramblings, recognisable but…
A heavenly gift, enhancing knowledge
Loving guidance, a golden treasure
Enlightenment, a mapped guide to rainbows end
Enhancing resolve, furtherance, rewards unknown.

Open up your heart, your mind, your soul
Lay it bare, the world's your oyster
Suffering fools with light-hearted reverences
Weary of all who'd take advantage
Their only allegiance, embedded deep, deep within
Listening attentively, to inner, inner, intuitive wisdom.

Life Ever-Changing

My life as yours is ever-changing
A wind, bending and twirling, around and around
Whilst the humble Magnifique Willow
Bows proudly to its aggressor, gracefully bending
With such tender flexibilities to the onslaught
Of mighty gales and gusting winds.

Are we not all mutable commodities?
Simplistic in forms, temporary inhabitant refugees upon these plains
Though we possess an intellectuality
Of embryonic proportions, we still talk ineffectually and supposedly, talk the talk, and walk the walk
Though it's nothing to be proud of or to shout about
While our level of understanding is minuscule at best.

Even microscopical details revealing
A new world to explore and to understand
As does the cosmic skies and the unimaginable unmanifested plains
In truth and reality, we sit, extremely precariously
Upon a precipice, an overhanging cliff
As we tumble around and around, in an unmindful stupor.

It's time we woke up from our slumberous pursuits
Stop being the lemmings with suicidal tenancies
In acceptance of our weaknesses, irrational fears, and susceptibilities
To stand tall, to bow gracefully, to the oncoming winds
Walking always in mindfulness's, respectfully tolerant to all
Bending inconspicuously with love and compassion, while radiating goodwill and generosity straight from your heart.

Light Is the Darkness

Alone in the darkness, a vacuum of light and hope
Embedded within emptiness, limitless nothingness
Floating, floating, drifting in the dark, peaceful unmanifested commune's, essences of souls
Not a sound nor reflection, pitch blackness, all around.

Incredulous, indescribable, unimaginable darkness
Not a glimmering, a flickering of tangible light
Invisible energies and light, streaming passed, through and through

One's spiritual essence gliding effortlessly, effortlessly on.

Conscious awareness, virtually non-existent, a bare smidgeon observed
Karma working, while you're submissively resting, unconscious, deep, deep asleep
A formless essence, a bubble afloat in bitch blackness, cosmic, oceanic sea
Bathing in loves, swirling blissful ecstasies.
Many, many eons, swiftly passing, before time, space, and one's essence is an awakened reality
Resting in peaceful silence, with your nearest, and dearest
Though you'll never sense or know it, they're there, encompassing everything, nevertheless
Waiting, waiting, imminent recycling – rebirth!

Seek Within

Not to the stars, the heavens
The cosmos, do I turn
Nor to the manifested, unmanifested planes
Complexities, far, far beyond
Our beliefs, understandings, or imaginings
Light and dark matter and many, many particles in between.

Not to the world's infrastructure, frustrating sufferings
Humanity owes to its human incompetent, foolhardy antics
But to the essence, of one's soul
Our spiritual home, where love, peace, and harmony, patiently linger, awaiting our dawning
Whist sharing the complexities of humankind's unwritten history
Reluctantly inhabiting a once empty shell, playing host to its symbiotic, soulful essence.

Not for the faint-hearted, who'll fear to wander, to tread the wildernesses

Darkened, shadowy recesses of the inner soul, the intricacies within the infamous egocentrically incarnated presence, Hades upon earth
While searching unknown abysses within, a layered inferior biologically motivated intellect
Peeling back many, many unfamiliar layered territories, layer by layer, to one's ordained destiny
True unfettered, unwavering peace, within the emptiness of nothingness – enlightening, finally the soul!

Matter

Manifested light matter, the illusionary
Materialistic worlds we know, we love
Dark matter, the unseen, invisibly cloaked
Hidden from perceptions, our reality
The unmanifested, spiritual plane.

Where our symbiotic essences of souls
Returns, when old age, reoccurring death, the human host, to dust must go
Revisits the oceanic unmanifested collective seas
Absorbing, processing, learning, revitalising energies.

Though the spiritual essence, the astral body
Floats free, free, out, out, of its protected, now empty shell
Enjoying the pleasures of true uncompromising realities
Swimming in esoterically darkened, unseen, unmanifested planes.

Floating free as a bird upon the wing
In prevailing winds through timeless space
Tethered to symbiotic human's host, by a swirling silvery cord
Freely wandering the unmanifested plane's, intrinsically designed dark matter.

Not Written in Stone – Yet!

A manifestation of an illusionary self-regulating ecosystem
Blowing unharmoniously with humanism
Changing moments of materialistic nocuous
Clumsily motivated intellectuals, unrealistic desires, and dreams.
A future's inconsequentiality, continuous fluxion
Destinations dawning, journeys without endings
Nothing ever staying, staying the same,
Drifters' realities, sliding indecorous plates.

Diminishing simmering possibilities, crying out in convoluted agonistic pain
Twisted emotional, desires, and unworthy dreams
Emotional anxieties, screaming loudest, supremo's nightmarish unimaginable fear of all
Swiftly striking viper's, an uncorked reality.
Futures unfolding, fumes intensifying in warm climatic winds
Sliding realities, a pendulum's swing
Matchings, not in harmony, to our beating whims
Instigators we are, disconcerting behaviours, without malice, perpetrators, never the less.

Every action, inaction, deliberate or not
Populous explosion triggering a reaction to a caused effect
Simulating responses, karmically inducements
Of short-sighted-drifters, unsatisfied dreamers, and imaginings.
Umbrellas won't stop the down-pouring wrath
Of a mutating ecosystem, unlikely revenge
Though in truthful reality, it's protection it seeks
Like a mutating virus, it will strike, again, and again, unless we wake, casting off our unworthy impromptu naivety!

One Moment

There is only one moment
That moment is now
In the duality
That is the manifested
The unmanifested planes.
The only planes we're privy to
Though others, in existence too
Beyond the realms of inconsequentialities
Of our reality and far, far, out
Of reach, of our manifested illusionary now.

Essences of our souls
Oft' traverse these barriers
Visiting unknown universal territories
In far, far, off planes
Manifestations of the collectives consciousnesses.
Interwoven within or out there, there, many trillions
Trillions, of light-years from here, from now
Far, far beyond the furthest stars
Or perspective universes envisaged or imagined
Beyond known universal boundaries.

Differing times, space, and realities
New dimensional truths
The other half of this duality, maybe
Of the manifested and unmanifested planes
Vaguely known to our, ill-perceived reasonings.
So, easily crossing territoriality boundaries
While possessing spiritualistic, not supper human abilities
Traversing time, space, and outer rims
To unknown, unquantifiable realities, flying free
In one's astral body, while remaining in this moment –
always, now!

Our Destiny Choices

Master, why is it my prayers
Go unanswered, my words
Never heard, though spoken echoing
Across time, space, and spiritual avenues.
No one answers, never comes
Not even an angel to guide me
In my neediness, to end my sufferance
Upon this unearthly, demonically possessed, manifested plane.

My pupil; it amuses me, amuses me, to think
That God/Allah, with courage and great wisdom, created it, thus
Giving us intellectual abilities?
To think, think, for ourselves.
The world, time, space, the manifested
The unmanifested infrastructures, veins running deep, deep into the substructures of true reality
Far, far complex than tiny intellectual abilities can ever conceive, fathom, or understand.

We make our destinies, over many lifetimes, maybe
God/ Allah set the boundaries; karma is the servant
A naturally controlled environment, teaching us
Valid ethical and moral values of heavenly wisdom.
A pendulum swing, back and forth, right from wrong, good from bad
Our choices to make, which way to swing
Or to choose a differing path, the middle road
Were little friction or disturbances felt, betwixt pairs of opposites, extreme to one another.

Look around, around you, all you see, hear, touch
Smell and senses, all created by God/ Allah
Teaching us to thrive, to survive, to grow, to become one
In harmony with the true reality of nothingness.

Not of the duality existent, here and now
God/Allah is always watching o'er us, by night, by day
Watching us making fools of ourselves, in sequential, non-devotional displays
Of mindlessness, carelessness, and egocentricity's – when will we ever learn?

Within

Peace and happiness
Waits for us, in our spiritualistic essences
Out of sight, there, there, inside our open-handed grasp
Search, thus, the wisdom's, loving blissfulness within.

Beating harmonious, cosmic enthused, energetic resonating waves
Natural perfectionism, unveiling, unfolding
One by one, through humanity's elite
Devoted, warriors of modern, scientific times.

Lighting up the world, one day
Converging sunlight from distant galaxies
Explosive, impacting upon us, one by one
Beaming light waves, illuminations to come.

Though, for this singular moment, moment of time
Exploration's steering subjectively, to the microcosm within
Peeling back the layers, of delusionary perceptions, illusive
Enlightenment, the blissful, nothingness, of true peaceful happiness's within.

Peaceful Tranquillity

One in the silence
The silence of oneness
Mindful, instinctual nature
One's consciousness, all prevailing.

Calming, tranquillity
A stilling, a graceful serenity
Not a sound uttered or perceived
Influential disturbances, a dream.

Left behind, to lurk
In the shadowy depths
Where brave men oft' fear to tread
Venturing forth, reaping, reaping, harvesting.

No rattling chains to speak of
No thoughts, feelings, or emotions
Senses pacified, dulled, indolent
An all becalming, oceanic sea.

Focusing, mind, body, and soul
To inner and outer perceptive realities
Upon the manifested planes
Of inherent natural abilities.

An enlightening magnificence, unveiling invisibility
Of one's true, self-nature
Awareness's, mindfulness's, and consciousness
A clarifying undiluted tranquillity – the heavenly peace within!

Picked from the Dust

Pick me, up, up
Out of the crumbling earth
The shadowy dust, the dirt

Let me flirt with life's dangerous imaginings.
From out of the cinereous ashes
My once humanistic shell
Now free to fly solo, solo, free-spirited
Freely, freely, swiftly, gracefully through the air.

My body, a simplistic vessel
For my in-descendant soul
A once empty shell, biologically
Mechanically, hopefully, sound.
A lifetime of arduous learning
For my spirited soul
My opposite number of dualities, a wilfully demonic
Incarnated, hellish self-creation, self-centred, fool.

Mindfully dwell there, not too often
It'll do you no good
Imposing its will upon you, a headache you'll see
Incessantly chattering, inside your head.
Flowing, streaming impromptu
Desire, anxieties, wishes and unfulfilled dreams
Echoing endlessly, unforgivingly
For as long you're an incarcerated symbiont
A prisoner, to a self-centred, incompetent fool!

Rippling Waves

Throw a stone into murky waters, deep
Of a pond, deep space, or oceanic seas
See the rippling foundations, precipitously forming
Violently expanding, explosive energies sensed
Escaping confines, while finding least resistive paths
Sound, light, thermal, fast, slow, not integral differences
Reactions to a cause, knock on devastations, and effects, far,
far-reaching, imagined or perceivable.

A volcanic eruption, a stone tossed, into a pool
Supernovas in outer space, a volcanic eruption, a tsunami undersea
Hypocentre or ground zero of wavy ripples
Rippling eternal waves of unbound potentialities
Three hundred and sixty degrees, turn around
Chain reactions, expanding energies
Large or small, the rise, the fall, extensive harmonic resonating consistencies

Diminishing frequencies and energetic waves, recognisable, all known and unknown types
Reflecting disturbances by many, many, external influences
A rock in a pond, a shore upon oceanic seas
A comet, moon, star, in cosmic oceans deep
Always circling, expanding explosivity, or implosively
Cycling waves of life, and death, cause, and effect
Simplistic complexities, embedded theories of everything – karma's laws!

Serenity

It is a human pleasure
To sit calmly in a world
Full of opposites
In meditational silence
Quiet, still and in a meditative, mindful, peaceful state.
Floating gently through
The multi-layered complexities
Of one's mind, into the caverns
Deep, deep, down, and down
Inwardly searching for the essence of one's very own soul.

Beneath the cumbersome egoistical minds
Fanciful trickery, laying trap upon trap to impeded
My pure mindful rest, at all, and any costs
As I unveil a wondrous, blissfully warm, and cosy place
Restfully calming and very, very darkened emptiness.

While fear a non-existent reality, down, down here, in the dark recesses of my mind
For deeper in, am I, than poor misguided, influentially gifted Egoist's game full play
Where desires, dreams, and material wealth
Have no value, no meaning, meaning here.

In the depths, I rest in the peaceful emptiness
Stretching, stretching out before my empty mind
For still are they, not a reflected sound or light
No echo, no pain, how could there be, no human senses prevailing here
Beyond the shadows, in my blissful solitude
In calm serenity, no effort needed, but to let go, let go
Of flowing life forces that are my breath and my ever slowing beating heart
While my aura reaches, out and out, far, and wide, reaching the stars and the heavens
Lands across, oceanic seas and the cosmic waves, way, way beyond.

Sending a warm and glowing embracing wave of generated loving energy
Compassion rare, to touch, to touch
Hearts and soul of so, so many, many
Irrespective of need, a little loving-kindness to give, to receive
My gift, to all there has ever been, is, or will ever be
The essence of my soul, as is yours, pure unadulterated
As I abide in the peaceful harmonies I've searched for so, so long
Letting go, go of my earthly desires, wishes and dreams
Passing beyond old forgotten and forsaken egoistical mind, to dwell in the reality that is the Peace Within.

Simplicity?

Life is never as simple
As it seems
While thoughts, feelings, and emotions
Are swelling ripples across the surface waters of a pond
In simple but distractions
To that ever-lasting peace
The one and only you.

Count the barriers if you can
They're there for sure, they are
Understand them for what they truly be
And let them go, go, if you can
To drift swiftly, by and by
Under the bridge
And far, far out to sea.

We mustn't dwell upon these streaming's
Of ceaseless demonic follies hither too
For they'll always hide the truth from you
And never give you any, any peace or clarity of mind
Abandon ye every single one
The senses only protection for our symbiont's empty shells.

Quell your innermost fears and doubts
All thoughts of what you're about to do
Dig deeper than you've ever done before
And venture into unknown scary, scary, territories for you
With brave heart beneath the egoistical groins
And all that its deluded perceptions make you, you
To reset as one in harmony with heavenly emptiness.

No sound, vision, smell, or reflections, too
All gone at last, beneath the bridge to sea, to sea
Leaving you in a quiet, relaxing, desirable place to be
Where all is calm, peaceful and love fulfilled

Dissimilar to the torrential influxes of demonic lightning flashes
Delusional glimpses of happiness and minuscule pleasures, always draining upon your soul
To reside in heavenly blissfulness, in loving peace, in harmony with all.

Simplistic but Effective

How the seasons come and go
The leaves falling, down, down
To the ground in autumn tides
To renew their stately prowess
Amongst the early buds of spring.

We follow like footsteps in the snow
Or desert winds lifting sands
Or oceanic waves pounding upon the shores line
The clouds that rise and fall as rain
Minuscule particles of homemade dew.

A mist, a cloud, drifting hither and thither
Upon the variant prevailing air undertones
Streaming across the cosmic skies
Returning to earth as simplistic rain
A little maybe or perhaps, a torrential downfall.

The cycle of life, death, and rebirth
Continuously flowing in natures good time
As a dance, to the climatic variational themes
Over hills, valleys, mountain peaks and pastures new
Changing, changing, now and again to snow.

How our lives doth follow suit,
The treasured sound of a new-borns cry
The smile of a person of maturity
Struggling now, but with a certain grace and dignity
While courting couples, casually walk, hand in hand.

It's a wondrous present; this is to behold
Gods nature park here upon earth
As we oft' tumble about spasmodically
Across the manifested plains, no less
That is to us, a simple playground!

Solitude

Are you lonely when you're all alone?
With no one, ever to talk with, but the monthly
Grocery deliveryman, who stops, for a quick moment
While removing groceries from his baskets, before he's gone, gone, gone.

Quiet isn't the word when you're seated all alone
Staring at the ceilings, staring at the walls
Living every regurgitated moment, thought, fear, and emotion
Materialising unwittingly inside, inside, your head.

Do you, really want to cry, to scream out, out, aloud?
Bang your head, head, hard up against the wall
Hoping it'll stop the unregulated flowing chatter
Tormenting, thoughtless, deliberations, swirling around and around, inside your lonesome head.

Stop, listen, listen, and learn, from the silences
It's a rarity in modern-day society
For it to be, so peaceful, for you to be alone
Whilst screaming, streaming unfettered thoughts, rally implicitly inside, inside, your head.

The answer to all, isolated doubts, fears, thoughts, feelings, and emotions – simplicity itself
For the I, as in me, is a created illusion, a birth defect, one might hesitate to say
Controlling your delusions, laughing at a fool, as opposed to you controlling it

Giving you the heebie-jeebies, running amuck, inside,
inside, your head.

Sit down, down, calmly, calmly relaxing, listen to the
silences, a piece of heavenly bliss, a pleasure after all
Enjoy it while ye can, whilst controlling your thoughts,
feelings, and emotions
The five senses, too; whilst putting the I, as in me, to bed
Discovering waiting, waiting there, true peace, harmony, and
happiness's, right there, there inside your head.

Spinning Tops

I sense the world beneath my feet
Spinning, spinning, around and around
As my mind whirls, ever, ever faster, and faster
To catch up with it, I think.

My mind spins like a spinning top in ever-increasing circles
Swirling about precariously in my head, making me a little,
little dizzy, dizzy, now, and again
It's neither contemplated, wished for, nor my good fortune
To be out of control, control, of one's very own facilities.

Whilst my little demonic voices, chatter endlessly in
whispers, whispering sweet nothings, nothings, into my sea
of thoughts
Whilst jump around and around, cheering joyously in sheer
delightfulness's to proceed
Wittingly, to jeer, to stimulate this madness, on, and on
Until I wobble, wobble, and falter, falling, down, down,
down upon my knees.

It may be their good fortune, now, to spin their pathetic
webs, but
I can play devil's advocate, too, to those little demonic
whisperers

Having a trick or two, well-hidden out of sight, up my sleeves
Laying a hidden trap to turn the tables and laughers into disastrous connotations for them.

I have been practising whilst honing my meditational skills
In recognition of the control, it gives me, over my innermost thoughts, feelings, and emotions, too
To quell those mischievous rascals forever, scurrying around and around, in my head
Giving me blissful peace and happiness everlasting, in mindful harmonies.

Symbiont

An empty shell, a symbiont host
A vessel, a vehicle for a soul
Freely moving, across all planes
Of a manifested illusionary world.

Sense, the minuscule movements
Of the spirit, astral body, the soul within
Adjusting karmically to challenging winds
Eternally unfolding, causes and effects.

God/Allah's automated creation, a gift,
Symbionts enduring, a duality of wits
Working togetherness, harmonising entities
An illusionary unperceived realty.

A state we're all privy too, devotedly meditating
Calming the body, the spiritual entity within
Mindfully aware, of a free-flowing spirituality
Symbiotic twins, synergies, fluidity within.

Soul working in harmonising rhythmical flowing dances
Tunefully harmonising with inexplicable conceptualities
Whilst seeking, true peace and harmony in an unmanifested emptiness's, an unknown realm
Despite alluring temptations, discovering within – pure essence of soul.

The Eyes Watch

The heavens above, the unmanifested plains
Watch intently, as we tumble around and around
In ignorance, while following idiotic guidance of a lesser guide
Ignoring unwisely, the wisdom taught by prophets of old.
Handed down to them by the truly graceful
Omnipotent one, who in his wisdom gave us the precious gift of intellectual abilities
To use, to learn, to make the right choices, not only for ourselves
But for the good of humanity and all God's creatures here.

How ashamed of us, must God/Allah be
For surely, he grimaces whilst wishing to turn his back upon us
As his eagle eyes watch on, ever perplexed at our stupidity
Unfolding before him, a blanket unrolled, full of sorrow, sorrow, sorrow.
Since all God-fearing religions and agnostics, atheists too
All preach or believe in the same very words and rhetoric
Spoken for many, many millenniums
And yet, our spiritual development has been less than that of a flea's.

Who jumps up and down from one life to another?
Doesn't care nor worries, if it can suck
The blood from a pound of flesh
To saviour momentarily while fulfilling its temporary needs.
It's time to learn from lessons repeatedly failed

Stop our petty squabbling's and distorted childish games
Creations of man's inabilities to comprehend
In his innocence or ignorance, no matter which.

Standing firm like the mighty oak
Who breaks its bow yielding not, to heeded gales warnings?
To stop the slaughterous barbaric onslaughts, putting down one's shiny arms
Aside, our stupendous pride, and the little differences we have
For they aren't so great, but our cultural, religious, and human influences
As taught by man, while in similar inherited mind-sets
Seeking, therefore, from the dark, dingy shadows, the power over their minions
Through the distorted, unhindered, emotive influences of a braggartly contemptuous coward, the real hell on earth – the Egoic mind!

The Line in the Sand

There is a line drawn
Clearly across the well-trodden sandy
Shores of the cosmic seas
Pounded and beaten into submissive docility by stormy seas
Wave upon wave of tempestuous batterings
As the mind reels, rolls, and shakes
To its very essence, its spiritual being.

Heaving, twisting, swirling to the ceaseless desires
Needful to please, to fulfil, the irrational nocuous wishes
Of an overbearing master's dreamful imaginings
Never-ending, never cessing, a constant draining flow
Drifting throughout the mindlessness
Confused and battle-weary inevitabilities
Soul destructors of devils incarnate whimsical ultimatums.

Begone, begone, I say, begone, beast of the devil, beast of hades
My mind has junk enough to blockade the flow
Without your persistent, infectious abominations
To stir up my souls, impediments to my mindfulness's endeavours
Nor the act of love or pleasurable fulfilment of its fruitfulness
But the garish temptations and a once eaten apple
The malicious, impromptus, sinful demeanour that stirs up the corrupt emotional attachments to all.

The line marked in the sands on the cosmic shores
Is for a virtuous reason, not a bluff or a ruse
Cross its boundaries at your peril, reaping demoniac rewards
To dwell upon this plain, for as long as ye will
Until you, your decisiveness prevails to knock upon realities door
Residing thereafter, eternally in enriching true love, peace, and compassion, harmoniously one!

The Mirage of Perception

The rain and sun join hands and clap
Emotionally embracing in mystifying, enchanting
Arrays of delight, arching across the mixed emotional skies
Bringer of such joys and happiness, in a wondrous magical rainbow effect
Of cherished moments, memories, warming electrifying
Whilst old wife's tales and folk law, speak brazenly
Whilst foretelling the miseries, melancholy, and many, many broken, bleeding hearts
Befalling, millions and millions of innocence
Whose faith in dreams was indeed their one and only misguided crime.

Unveiling, fanciful, unrealistic fairy-tale endings
Of buried golden pots of treasures, if only, if only

Waiting, waiting unearthing, under rainbow's invisible cloak
Whilst boundaries flux and wane, in continuously drifting tides
Of heartfelt beats of shattering, splintering hopes of unfulfilled dreams
Sobbing, weeping, and crying in buckets loads
Bowing heads in gullible shamefulness, whilst trying, trying, desperately to hold on, on
Whilst the serrated edge blade, of our twisted
Egotistical whimsical selves, thrusts deeper, deeper, in increasingly, agonising unnecessary volleys of masquerading tomfoolery
Slashing, cutting, deeper, deeper into one's heart, one's soul.

Foolhardy to dream, maybe, but not wrong, never wrong
Dreams oh, dreams, such wondrous dreams, dreams of a better life
For you, your children, and your nearest, your dearest
In a world, rife with disease, manipulative infestations of sufferance
Far, far worse than any, any, killer, killer disease ever could be
Dreams are just that, dreams, imaginings of the Egotistical mind-set
A mirage, born of one's ill-conceived irrational perceptions
Be kind, be generous to one's self, seek ye not the rainbow's end
But the true reality, true Peaceful Bliss Within.

Time

I am an essence of soul
So, too, are you
Possessing no gender
No emotional promptitude or behaviours, human frailties
Distractions upon predestined paths.

Interwoven, entwining spiritualities

A drifting collective, oneness
In a vast wilderness
Unmanifested collective's essences of souls
Dualities upon existent universal planes.

Shooting unseen, effortlessness through time, and space,
a lightning bolt
Faster than sound, faster than light
Perfections of consciousnesses
Synchronicity, harmonising simplicities
Beautiful, balancing onenesses, of time and space.

Adhering to scaled indeterminacies
Inherent inexplicable wave principles
Home of dualities, time and of space
Manifested and unmanifested planes
Of illusionary perceptions of realities.

Born to cycle, endless challenging waves, of life, of death
Gleaming bright, a star born today, gone tomorrow
One perfect goal, many, many, questions
Unanswered, to meditate upon, while time flashes passed
Unaltering dimensional space, learning curve humongous,
for embryonic dualities, humankind, and souls, alike.

Too Late?

To sense, to touch, to see
To hear, to taste and to smell
But to love oneself as another
Is it truly, truly on the cards
In today's social spheres and realms of plausible possibilities
And our undignified layered structures.
The senses guide and protect us
Through the screaming torrents of indulgent temptations
And the body, from pending dangers
In a world full of hostilities
A life full of unwanted fears, anxieties and want haves

And a trail of unnecessary pressurised insanities.
The senses are a good thing, I think
To preserve and protect, at least
Are one of nature's unwisely forgotten creations
Whilst human minds pull together
Whilst it perceives and to give the manifested
A form of delusionary acceptability.

We're forever evolving, into new unconceivable entities
That may well, well, take your breath away
And the root causes of our tormentors
Uncooperative insolence, unworthy symbolic displays
Only befitting a child's, childish tantrums
Whilst letting us stop all our nonsensical dreams.

As we stopped to take stock
Of a world, full of shattered and unimaginable wishes
Unrealistically impossible ambitions of impermanence
To take heed of the many, many warnings
Of pending danger, before it's too late, to swiftly reconsider
The realistic outcome of our once, enviable dreams.

Why Hide

Why do we hide
Skulking there, on the fringes
Amongst the personas
Of shadowy materialistic values
Egocentricities personified
Of a warped, ill-perceived sense of reality.

Why not pridefully seek
True peace and reality
Shown in their spiritualistic wisdom,
By the ancient prophets, of old
Prideful of our duties
Human host to the symbiotic soul within.

There to learn, to enrich us

Beyond wildest imaginings
Beyond our wildest dreams
Whilst we in our inconceivable
Wisdom, seek only self-gratifications
Whilst rampaging across forbidden, untouched lands.

Enriching our materialistic, desires and dreams
Through ignorances and short-sightedness
Detrimentally harmful to the essence, our soul
Whilst unforgivingly perpetuating infinite motions
Endless karmically chosen wanderings upon the wilderness
Of time, of space, upon manifested planes.

Whilst the essence of time, wasted, self-indulgently imposed
Accounting for more years than eternally imaginable
Drifting, drifting sands upon deserted dunes
Why, was the question, the answer
Simplistic in nature, but complexities abound
An enduring reason, to keep us tethered, eternally entwined!

Value of the Peace Within

I am but a humble human
My body a vessel for my soul
From where the words
Flow freely as a stream from the unmanifested collective
To the manifested illusionary world.

I frown upon my weaknesses
My human senses, thoughts
Feelings and emotions, too
A never-ending flowing stream of sufferance
Swaying us, relentlessly to do it's bidding too.

Referencing the many, many, names throughout history
It is the true and only beast within
Preventing, blocking, sidestepping, our every endeavour of fulfilling
Our true purpose upon these manifested soils
To seek, to find the true undelusional precepted reality.

How deceitful is its human nature?
To hamper, to devour every shred or inclination
To seek, to find, to dwell in true blissfulness
A glimpse of heavenly natures, the unadulterated bliss
The true oneness, the peace within.

Seek to stem the flowing tides
Waves upon wave of temptations to illusionary happiness
Whilst barricading and blocking our paths to reality and one's true soulful destiny
Circumventing its carelessness, is the challenge to enlightenment, with pure-hearted, devotional dedication and to let go
Let go, of the only infestation, demonic incarnated hauntings, now and forever more.

Our Ultimate State

Lift up your head, walk with prideful steps, raise your spirit, your soul
Rejoice up, up, in clouded nightly skies
Flying free amongst twinkling, shimmering stars
Glimmering emanations, waves of healing, light energy
Drifting down, down, gracefully upon symbiotic hosts.

Moonbeam blessings, heavenly gifts
Descending angels, heartfelt particles
Loving gentile touches upon one's brow
Spiritual energies, flowing through, once empty shells
Deep concentrations, a quest fulfilled awakening coiled serpent, rooted deep.

Discovering the beauty of one's wondrous symbiotic host
Graceful movements, through dense atmospheric influences
Impediments to spirit, and host alike, imperceptible
Invisible complexities, to life and limb
Confining, restrictions for dancing
Known essences, ripening, maturing within.

Fluctuating energies radiating out, out, from within
Feelings, sensing one's symbiotic hosts fluidity
Entwining, endearing motions, in synchronised harmonies
Human potential, evolving to an ultimate state
Body and soul, moving closer, closer, together, balancing differences
Becoming one, pure energy in the oneness of emptiness.

The Destroyers

Look no further; we're the scurvy, the destroyers
Servants of plagues, pestilences, and sufferings
Upon once beautiful, dense fertile lands
Famine creators, crustaceans encroaching across plains
Responsibility ours, all ours, ours.
Spreading wildfires, no forethought, forbearance
Planning, accountability, just naive misguided insensibilities
Breath holders, ostrich heads, deep, deep, into sands
Hoping; waiting, waiting, alarm bells, won't echo throughout the land.

Irresponsible breeding, rats to the slaughter, marching
Marching to the same, merry old tunes
Affordability question, asked, not answered
Grains of sand, falling, falling, through hourglasses' eye, one by one, by one
The end nigh, or an epiphany, a moment, an awakening
Celebration time, rolled out red carpets, across the land
Carrying, long lost, forgotten, maimed, weeping, refugee's, to safety, for what, power-hungry inhumane men's ideologies

Unnecessary butchery of wild animals, almost extinct, gone, gone, gone.
We smile disbelievingly, whilst uttering the words, 'It'll never be!'

Selfish, unintelligent, suffering a fool's complacency?
Lacking intellectual abilities to envisage, to forward plan,
for a better peaceful world, a harmonious place to be
Most, not all, sit relaxing, cosily in comfy armchairs
Not a word, nor opinion whispered beneath their unhealthy breaths
No thoughts flowing through tiny minds, nothing, nothing, at all, except in silent echoing undertones
'Not my problem, it's up to the rich, the powerful.'
Isn't the answer, nor is, a few trillion dollars either, though it may help, a little
Whilst the world goes on fighting, arguing, amongst itself
Sidestepping the true, natural, devil's advocate in a well-oiled, well-rehearsed, ill-organised house of tumbling cards.

Entity of Evolution

Let us rediscover, bringing them
To the forefront of our minds
The true values of humanity
Embracing the spirit of oneness.

Purity of heart, mind, and soul
One family, upon these manifested plane
One with all life, roaming
Upon these manifested illusionary planes.
Let the rain shower down upon us
Washing away, way, our waves of tears
Tears of sadness, of forlorn hope
Of sufferance's, spawned self-gratifications.

Paying heed to past mistakes, to walk
Forever, together in peaceful mindfulness's

In tolerant, behavioural respectfulness to all
Upon these manifested illusionary planes.

Embracing evolution's nurturing, to grow, blossom and bloom
Becoming one, in mind, body and spirit
A shining light, a new amalgamated spiritual
An entity, harmonising, all-encompassing peaceful – love!

Drowning in Dreams

Confusion reigns upon unmanifested soils
Karma, overwhelmed with many, many requested
Desires, wishes and dreams
Unmanifested collectives, thrown into disarray.

Swamped in cosmic oceanic sea
Full of unfulfilled
Desires, wishes, and dreams, whilst karma wrestles
Relentlessly, struggling; overwhelmingly overloaded.

Temper your wishes, your dreams
Ease the burden; karma must rest
As you would, if you could, when you're tired
Exhausted from impromptu requests.

No wonder, when everyone's selfishly seeks
To harvest materialistic fulfilling ephemeral pleasures
Whilst, only obtaining, unsatisfactory
Rapturous, interluded moments of felicity.

Now, a stagnating, festering quagmire of inappropriately requested prayers
A resolution at hand, to regulator the flow
Treading the middle road of mindfulness
Curtailing ever-flowing, oceanic seas of dreams.

Self-Perpetuating

How cruel is one's mind?
How cruel is yours?
Full of self-perpetuating, hypnotic
Wishes, desires, and dreams.
Guilty are we
Who seeks, oft' in vain
Self-sustaining, ritualistic echoings
Fiendish, incomprehensible, conceptual realities.

Self-absorbing, unremitting
Egos influencing, conceitedly flowing, impromptu dreams
Hog tying, bound and tethered
Upon this manifested plane.

Self-servicing, it may be, detrimentally
Affecting, deluded, gullible, embryonic souls
Confusion reigns down upon, new, once empty shells
Born, yesterday's new symbiotic hosts.

Why? Why? do these, soon, duped, misguided
Minds of human children, grow to lose
Their innocence, their inquiring, virtuous, all-encompassing
Egotistical minds, to seek momentary illusionary happiness?

Counting Blessings

Why discriminate amongst ourselves?
Tearing strip after strip off one another's back
Leading not, to any formed reconciled peace and harmony?
Are we full of misconceived ideologies?
Not smart enough, intellectual enough to see?
Inner faults and failings, lying undetected, adjacent to
misconceived ideas – however, conceived.

Many, many differing religions, philosophies, and cultures
Differing traditions and ceremonies

Not surprising Earth, as experienced
Is in crisis, though most, bury forethoughts,
unimaginatively with their heads, deep, deep, into sands of time
Than reluctantly face truths, their concerns, and their nightmares
Slowly decaying, until we stand together, united family.

We fight, bicker, and argue, religion our excuse, though scriptures speak so, wisely
Preferring to play sinful, stupid egotistical games
Than face undeniable truths of reality
Stop now, I say, stop our petty squabbling, it's long overdue
Join united humanity, a loving, caring race, projecting strong overtones, sensibilities to the oneness of humanity
Counting our blessings, not – disease-ridden festerings.

Invisible Walls

Open up your heart, your soul
Embrace the world, all thereupon
Light waves shining radiances, down, down
Gracing your ever, ever-loving presence.

No, more, no more, invisible walls
Knock them down, gone, gone, to dust
No more guarded, guarded secrets
Pure unadulterated, tender loving care.

Open up your heart, your soul,
Embrace the world, all thereupon
Let not poisons, flow, flow
Unguarded impetuosity.

Grace the world, now, now, as if, it is home
Your one, your only, passionate lover
See it grow, to blossom, to bloom
Flourishing heavenly, eternal, gifted light.

New Light Dawning

Looked in the mirror
To comb my hair
I saw a reflection
It was not me.

A face of gentile tranquillity
Staring back, back, at me
Radiating calming, loving, engrossing easiness
Eye's sparkling, a radiant, beaming, smiling light.

Words of perfection flowing freely, captivating waves
Guiding influences, love, and tenderness, rare
Telepathic communication, it must surely be
Streams of warming, heartfelt energies.

I've travelled wide and far, to be
Born entwining, your synchronised symbiont
Guiding, teaching, and to learn
Together with mindful oneness, in emptiness.

Dark matter merging into the light
Through nocuous gases, and symphonic
Waves of energies, many, many frequencies
Drifting intricacies, universal significances.

Let's embrace one another, in harmonious accord
Nurtured now, to blossom, to bloom
Gifting, a new wave to science, impending dawning
New light shining, upon modern pure, unadulterated esoteric mathematics.

Last piece of the cosmic jigsaw puzzle
Resolving the theory of everything
Absent upon manifested plane
Abundant in unmanifested, invisible dark matter.

Thinking of Me

You will think of me
Before you pass this very day
From this world to the next
I'm sure!

My words echoing, relentlessly
Through and through, crevasses of your mind
Your spirit, preparing, to let go, let go
Disconnecting from your earthly family.

Journeying forth and homeward bound
Absorbing, enduring cycles of life and death, once more
Into great unknowns, and on, and on, too
The unmanifested collectives' essences of souls.

I've warned you
Of incessant behavioural issues
Betwixt your dreams, fears
Desires and false imaginings.

Now, the test of time is here
It is your moment, now
My words, perhaps too late
For feasible considerations.

Preparations underway, for this moment, now
Fulfilment of your destiny
Learning upon, this rocky road, we walk
To love compassionately, at peace – within!

Ego!

I am Ego, your Ego
Your worst, nightmare
A bastard, an evolutionary
Spin-off, an interminable devotee

Cherishing, imaginatively challenging games.

I am, the one, the only
Platonical, influential demonic incarnation
Flooding minds with idiosyncratic sympathies
Plaques upon dualities
Upon manifested, unmanifested planes.

I reek perpetual, unabated infuriating havoc
I own you; I own these planes
Your idiosyncratic, ill-perceived realities
Running you ragged, for aeons
Your minds, into perpetual servitude.

I'll embrace every folly
Watch every squirm, dogs
Upon well-tethered leashes
Always dancing, always prancing
Foolish jesters of whimsical natures.

Watch you stamp pathetic marks into quicksand
Destroying lands, life extinct
In ignorance, you dream on, on
Never waking, never enlightened, never seeing, seeing,
beyond
Misty – falling rains.

Shameful

Sharpened axes, swung, down, down
Upon uncaring, damned if I do, damned if I don't, ideologies
Heads, rolling, rolling across planked bitter cold flooring
Falling heads, eyes popping out, echoing thuds of bouncing
hairballs, squirting severed arteries
Trailing, mingling congealing, swished, around and around
Fresh red blood curdling, upon drenched soaked floors
Shame be it, upon your head, shame upon mine.

Sit down, why don't you? Smug, tempestuous, in self-fulfilling, proclaiming gratitudes
Open your self-centred, stubborn minds, for once, instead of…
Intolerant, stupefying behaviours and ignorances
Listen, listen, sense, feel deep-rooted aboriginal intended meanings of my words
Universal Karma, broken down, down, in perpetual turmoil
Souls, many souls, in disarray upon these manifested planes
Communication damaged between dualities, planes waning, fast.

Spoken, scribed words, many inadequacies, taken too literally
Neither interpreted or understood, non-sensing feelings of the creator's emotional expressivity, heartfelt spiritual guidance
Cultural changes disregarded, not modernised, in an expanding global populace
Desperate moves, needed, brought caringly into line with tidal flowing, ever-changing wisdom
Responsibilities as caretakers of manifested, illusionary planes taken seriously, now virtually ignored
Indifferent attitudes, throwing karmas regulated unmanifested plane, into an infernal, in veritable spin.